IRISH POETRY
of Faith and Doubt

The Cold Heaven

By the same author:
Stalking after Time (1977)
High Sacrifice (1981)
Winter in Meath (1981)
Road, with Cypress and Star (1988)

Forthcoming:
The Stylized City: New and Selected Poems (1991)

Other Poetry Anthologies from Wolfhound Press:
Pillars of the House:Verse by Irishwomen, A. A. Kelly, ed.
Irish Poetry After Yeats, Maurice Harmon, ed.
Irish Poems for Young People, Quinn & Cashman, ed.

Forthcoming:
An Crann Faoi Bhláth/The Flowering Tree, Fitzmaurice & Kiberd, eds.
Sleeping with Monsters: Interviews with Scottish and Irish Women Poets, Rebecca Wilson, ed.

IRISH POETRY
of Faith and Doubt

The Cold Heaven

Edited by
JOHN F. DEANE

WOLFHOUND PRESS

Published in Great Britain 1991
First published 1990 in Ireland
WOLFHOUND PRESS
68 Mountjoy Square, Dublin 1.

British Library Cataloguing in Publication Data

The cold heaven: Irish religious poetry of
Faith and doubt.
1. Religious poetry in English. Irish writers –
– 1980 – Anthologies
I. Deane, John F.
821'.008'0382
ISBN 0-86327-144-8

Wolfhound Press receives financial assistance from The Arts Council (An Comhairle Ealaíon), Dublin, Ireland.
Cover Illustration: Detail from *The Holy Well* by William Orpen. By kind permission of The National Gallery of Ireland.

Cover design: Jan de Fouw
Typeset by Phototype-Set Ltd., Dublin
Printed by The Guernsey Book Company, Guernsey

CONTENTS

9

INTRODUCTION

There are many anthologies of religious poetry: Helen Gardner edited the *Faber Book of Religious Verse,* R S Thomas edited the *Penguin Book of Religious Verse* and a book appeared in 1980 from Villa Books in Dublin, called *Playing With Fire,* subtitled *A Natural Selection of Religious Poetry.* These are all very fine books. However, this anthology takes a narrower area of reference, Ireland, and a broader definition of what constitutes 'religious' poetry — poetry that has sprung from a reaction to religious beliefs, that is reaction in terms of acceptance, rejection or suspicion of the existence of a higher, unseen controlling power known as 'God'. I have excluded poetry that is merely devotional, that is a response in terms of service or homage to an already accepted God. (*The Deer's Cry,* Four Courts Press, 1986, has adequately covered this area). Included is poetry that rejects the existence of God, as this, too, is a reaction. But most important, perhaps, for this anthology are the poems that spring from hesitation, doubt and 'vacillation', as these appear to be the most common themes over the last hundred years. And finally, only those poems that succeed first as poems rather than mere versification, theologising or philosophising are included.

The poetry offered here conveys a strong, personal and individual response to belief in God; a great deal of devotional verse succeeds only in keeping that personal response at a safe distance. Richard Kell, in the sequence 'Heartwood', written in memory of his wife, wrote:

> *Ashes . . . What else?*
> *A breath for new lovers*
> *climbing Killiney Hill?*
> *A clear harmonic in some timeless music?*
> *Or, miraculously, your self*
> *distilled from all you were, knowing for ever*
> *'I', and even 'thou'? So many voices.*
> *One, echo and echo, keeps saying.*
> *'Ashes, what else?'*

11

Ireland is known for its tenacious belief in God: our early poetry, in Gaelic or Latin, is rich and lyrical in its response to that God, but that is not my concern here. The theme of this anthology is the vacillation, indignation and occasional rapture that Irish poets have experienced in their response, as poets, to religious faith.

Many of the poems here have been inspired by the contrast between professed beliefs and their actual practice; this satirical strain which took strength from Austin Clarke, appears in Richard Murphy's 'Largesse', and in the poetry of Paul Durcan and others. Writers like Frances Alexander have written very fine devotional verses and hymns; 'There is a green hill far away . . .' and 'Once in royal David's city . . . ' are hers, but her 'Moral Songs', and her 'Poems on subjects in the Old Testament' suffer greatly from a polemical bias. Her preface to the latter book says:

'The writer's wish would be to prolong the child's love of the glorious Old Testament stories, by throwing round them something of the poetical tinge which is attractive to almost every mind in opening youth; and thus to connect associations of quiet pleasure with the examples of holy life, and the doctrines of saving truth, which the Bible contains in such exceeding abundance.'

Such polemical writings abound in Irish verse, and there are cartloads of books in which a stock religious response is 'tinged' with the trappings of poetry; these works are ultimately boring in the extreme.

John Kells Ingram's 'Utinam Viderem' is the first Irish poem to urge a complete humanism, and this is done in traditional religous terms. Utinam Viderem is from a sonnet sequence that is filled with a great fervour, deeply stirred by the positivism of Auguste Comte; but the poet's vision of a Church that rejects 'imagin'd beings in the skies' and develops a universal humanism seems further off than ever in the 1990s. John Millington Synge and others wrote poems from the same viewpoint. William Allingham is heavily on the defensive, and sounds a certain petulant note now and again. His poetry is an example of the yielding attitude, the submission of the self to the Divine Will though doubts exist. This is a note that is heard often through the later poems in this anthology. John Todhunter, for instance, prays to God to take over his weak will and give him strength and courage; his use of the traditionally common technique of paradoxical imagery gives his poems strength; the apparent contradictions noted, only the yielding of faith brings peace. In the later poems of John Donne a great deal of this attitude prevails.

W B Yeats towers above his contemporaries in this respect as in so many others. It is strange to realise that so many were still publishing a trivial and old-fashioned religious versifying while Yeats was forging his poetry. With poets like Dora Sigerson Shorter, God is still a sentimental, somewhat sloppy figure, only occasionally reaching the interest of superstition, of the yarn we listened to as children huddling round a fire in the late evening. Katherine Tynan, however, achieves a simplicity and immediacy of language and imagery that is irresistible; in her work, too, there is the Marian imagery the Irish are so fond of, as Denis Devlin wrote, 'what we have best imagined is the Mother'.

Yeats's poetry is as complex in the religious sphere as in all others, moving from his interest in folk poetry in 'The Ballad of Father Gilligan' to his fully developed and personal statements in 'Vacillation'. His poem 'The Cold Heaven' is the first to introduce into Irish religious poetry a heart-rending questioning of the personal relationship between man and God. If Yeats's final position leaned more towards the religion of art itself, his struggle to achieve this position resulted in a series of superb poems. Underlying all his work is a quite traditional acceptance of Christianity; but his poetry deals with the complexity, the failures, the struggles and doubts that any person alert to the fire of human passion must experience when faced with the bland statements of Christian salvation. The fury of the questioning, the vacillation itself, give Yeats's poetry its depth and range.

And this is precisely where AE, George William Russell, fails. His practical and business-like turn of mind vanishes when he turns to God; his 'mystic' poetry remains in the realms of the fanciful. His acceptance of a primitive belief in the omnipresence of spirits from other levels of existence is exemplary of many esoteric religions, more common in Ireland now than ever before. But only the 'initiates' can experience the omnipresence of the other world; to the uninitiated the poems appear the result of a heightened imagination in the grip of an almost uncontrolled emotion; this poetry belongs more to the strange genre of esoteric propaganda.

In his history of *Ireland in the Twentieth Century,* John A Murphy has written: 'It must be remembered that from the 1930s to the 1950s the idea persisted that Catholic social principles could be applied successfully to Irish secular life and so help create a Christian society.' De Valera, in a speech of 1943, advocated 'a people satisfied with a frugal comfort' who 'devoted their leisure to the things of the spirit'. In those years the Catholic Church was somewhat hysterical about any form of communism or even socialism; 1932 was the year the 'Blueshirts' appeared, and the foundation and growth of Fine Gael offered the Irish counterpart to fascism, which in turn became associated with the social teachings of Pope Pius XI, a repressive Church, and groups, such as Maria Duce, bitter and vociferous critics of any form of liberalism. There was a response from the poets: Austin Clarke's *Night and Morning* was published in 1938; and in that year, too, appeared Louis MacNeice's *Autumn Journal*; in 1940 F R Higgins published *The Gap of Brightness*; and in 1942 W R Rodgers's *Awake* appeared. Kavanagh published *The Great Hunger* in 1942 and in 1945 Robert Farren published *The First Exile*, a long and unequal poem about Colmcille. Patrick Kavanagh's and Denis Devlin's poems called 'Lough Derg' were written about this time although not published until much later.

The influence Clarke and Higgins had on each other's poetic style did not extend to their religious outlook; Clarke's fierce commitment is not echoed by his jovial, unhurt contemporary. And in Clarke it is not God who is rejected but the destructive and reactionary attitude and dogmas of the Church. The clash between individual human growth and what Clarke saw as a fraudulent, hypocritical organisation is an extension of the Yeatsian struggle, but with Clarke it reached a level of intense and ongoing commitment. This austere, satirical, but wholly dedicated voice has had a powerful influence on later poets who have approached the religious question. In *The Great Hunger* Kavanagh's poor hero, Maguire, has a hunger for life that is totally unfulfilled; the Church has made life an evil thing, a valley of tears, mined with temptations, every signpost at every crossroads pointing towards Hell and damnation.

Louis MacNeice, growing up in a zealot faith which served only to lead men towards despair, also found despair in any form of humanism. With the terrors of the World War he found 'The Happy Future is a thing of the past', the relics of a faith once powerfully part of an everyday sensibility, lay dead; MacNeice's poetry charts his personal decline from faith to a gnawing emptiness. (I would have included many additional MacNeice poems here but for the exorbitant fees requested for reproduction — a regrettable trend in recent years, making the work of the anthologist dangerously uncommercial.) His friend, W R Rogers, attempted to bring back human joy into religion, to recover the primordial carelessness of a will thrown joyfully at the feet of the Divine; much of his poetry remains that of a celebrant rather than a questioner, and his resurrection sequence though magnificent, suffers from an occasional slip into sermonising.

And yet Padraic Fallon succeeded in a poetry that is religious in the traditional sense and is also perhaps our finest achievement; it succeeds because the trappings of faith so beloved in Ireland, the statues, the beads, the rules, the dogmas, are ignored, and the mystery of religion is fully internalised. His poems are profoundly personal, not side-tracked by any shifts in social conditions, and yet the poems remain fully alert to the ultimate mystery that remains in any religious faith. His is a clear, unsentimental eye, his religious poetry remains rich and valuable in a perennially satisfying way. Robert Farren, on the other hand, does not keep the sense of mystery; his poems take too much for granted. His long biography in verse of Colmcille/Columba sees the monks in Iona as living in an ideal state, somewhat as Clarke set up an idealised Ireland where man lived and worked as a unified human being. Of his poem, 'The Monks Work and Play', Farren wrote, '[it] fathers in one place what was separately and partially expressed in the songs of the monastic craftsman, and carries it on into the spirit of the man who guided and nurtured it all.'

More recent poetry tends to advocate one or the other side of the religious divide without hesitation. Thomas Kinsella's monk is a figure willing himself to find light in darkness; the imagery of the leap into an abyss of uncertainty outlined by Kierkegaard prevails in such poetry that is a determined willing towards faith. Seamus Heaney's 'Vacillation' approaches that of Yeats, 'In Illo Tempore' is in the persona of Sweeney, and this persona seeks the freedom and inspiration of art, while surrounded and impregnated by religious imagery. Richard Kell has produced a fine body of religious poetry that occasionally echoes the concerns of MacNeice. His poetry is intelligent and probing, exposing the limitations of puritanism. One of his books was *The Broken Circle,* a title which, as well as referring to the tragic drowning of his wife in 1975, symbolises the loss of the security of religious beliefs.

The poems presented in this anthology are poems in the English language tradition; the influences are basically those of the poetry of England, America and Europe. Religious poetry in the Irish language has a generally devotional tone, with the exception of a few contemporary writers; the tradition in Irish language religious poetry is a long one, going back to the early centuries of Christianity in this country. Hence the poetry in the Irish language is not relevant to the present study; a separate anthology of religious poetry in Irish would be of interest, but its thrust would differ greatly from that of the present anthology. I have, however, included some examples of religious poetry in the Irish language here to give the reader a sense, as it were, of its very distinctive and elegiac cast. A comparative and parallel anthology of religious poetry in the two traditions would indeed be of interest, but would, of its very nature, require quite different points of reference from those with which I began my selections for *The Cold Heaven.*

Cuireadh Do Mhuire

An eol duit, a Mhuire,
Cá rachair i mbliana
Ag iarraidh foscaidh
Do do Leanbh Naofa,
Tráth a bhfuil gach doras
Dúnta Ina éadan
Ag fuath is uabhar
An chine dhaonna?

Deonaigh glacadh
Le cuireadh uaimse
Go hoileán mara
San Iarthar cianda:
Beidh coinnle geala
I ngach fuinneog lasta
Is tine mhóna
Ar theallach adhainte.

Nollaig 1942

Invitation to Mary

Do you know, Mary/where
you will go this year/looking
for shelter/for your Holy
Child/when every door/is
closed in His face/by the hate
and pride/of the human race?

Grant an acceptance/of my
invitation/to an island in the
sea/in the remote West:/there
will be bright candles/
lighting in every window/and
a turf-fire/kindled in the
hearth.

Christmas 1942

(Máirtín Ó Direáin, *Selected Poems*, Goldsmith Press)

Teacht Chríost

Do ghlanas mo chroí anocht
Amhail mhnaoi do ghlanfadh
  a teach
Roimh theacht dá leannán dá
  fios:
A leannáin, na téirigh thart!

Do leathas doras mo chroí
Amhail fhear do-ghéanadh
  fleadh
Ar theacht i gcéin dá mhac:
A Mhic, is álainn do theacht!

Christ's Coming

I have made my heart clean
tonight/as a woman would
clean her house/before the
arrival of her lover on a
visit:/Lover, don't pass by!

I have opened the door of my
heart/as a man who would
prepare a feast/on his son's
coming from abroad:/Son,
your coming is lovely!

(Pádraig Mac Phiarais, *Filíocht Phádraig Mac Phiarais*, Clóchomhar)

Contemporary religious poetry is bitty – occasionally frantic – in its search for a more human faith; it is a bemused poetry, some of it springing from a generation stricken by the Vatican Council and its changes, and trying to find a new language for faith. The concerns of our time — violence, social injustice, the destruction of peoples by the greed of Super Powers, the attack on our traditional ways of living and dying — are perhaps concerns which our tradition of religious outlook and religious poetry has not learned to cope with yet.

It is my hope that this anthology presents rich and stimulating poetry, poetry that somewhat contradicts the common image of Ireland as unquestioning in its religious beliefs. Of course the poetry offers no final answers, no absolute certainties; perhaps it will serve to end with these lines from Paul Muldoon:

> *And I walk waist-deep among purples and golds*
> *With one arm as long as the other.*

JOHN F DEANE

JEREMIAH JOSEPH CALLANAN (1795-1829)

Mary Magdalen

To the hall of that feast came the sinful and fair;
She heard in the City that Jesus was there;
She mark'd not the splendour that blaz'd on their board;
But silently knelt at the feet of the Lord.

The hair from her forehead so sad and so meek,
Hung dark o'er the blushes that burn'd on her cheek;
And so still and so lowly she bent in her shame,
It seem'd as her spirit had flown from its frame.

The frown and the murmur went round thro' them all,
That one so unhallow'd should tread in that hall,
And some said the poor would be objects more meet,
For the wealth of the perfumes she shower'd on his feet.

She mark'd but her Saviour, she spoke but in sighs,
She dar'd not look up to the heaven of his eyes,
And the hot tears gushed forth at each heave of her breast,
As her lips to his sandal were throbbingly prest.

On the cloud after tempests, as shineth the bow;
In the glance of the sunbeam, as melteth the snow,
He look'd on that lost one; her sins were forgiven;
And Mary went forth in the beauty of Heaven.

———————

SAMUEL FERGUSON(1810-1886)

The Morning's Hinges

Where the Morning's hinges turn,
Where the fires of sunset burn,
Where the Pole its burthen weighty
Whirls around the starry hall;
Beings, wheresoe'er ye are,
Ether, vapour, comet, star,
There art Thou, Lord God Almighty,
Thou that mad'st and keep'st them all.

Where, on earth, battalioned foes
In the deadly combat close;
Where the plagues have made their stations,
Dropped from Heaven's distempered air;
Where within the human breast,
Rising hints of thought suggest
Sin's insane hallucinations,
Dread One, Thou art also there.

O most Mighty, O most High,
Past Thought's compass, what am I
That should dare Thy comprehending
In this narrow, shallow brain?
Yea, but Thou hast given a Soul
Well capacious of the whole,
And a Conscience ever tending
Right-ward, surely not in vain.

Yea, I'd hinder, if I could,
Wrath and pain and spilling blood;
I would tell the cannon loaded
'Fire not!' and the sabre stay
Mid-cut; but the matter brute
Owns its own law absolute;
And the grains will be exploded,
And the driven iron slay.

Deaf the nitre; deaf the steel;
And, if I the Man appeal,
Answer Soldier and Commander,
'We, blind engines, even as these,
Do but execute His plan,
Working since the world began,
Towards some consummation grander
Than your little mind can seize.'

What! does all, then, end in this,
That, amid a world amiss,
Man must ever be but parcel-
Imperfection? and the soul
Ever thus on poise between
Things contrarient, rest, a mean
Averaged of the universal

Good and ill that make the whole?

No, a something cries within;
No; I am not of your kin,
Broods of evil! all the forces
Of my nature answer No!
Though the world be overspread
With the riddle still unread
Of your being, of your sources,
This with sense supreme I know;

That, behoves me, and I can,
Work within the inner man
Such a weeding, such a cleansing
Of this moss-grown home-plot here,
As shall make its herbage meet
For the soles of angels' feet,
And its blooms for eyes dispensing
Light of Heaven's own atmosphere.

'Yea, what thou hast last advanced,
Creature, verily thou canst.'
(Hark, the Master!) 'Up. Bestir thee;
And, that thou may'st find the way,
Things inscrutable laid by,
Be content to know that I,
Hoping, longing, waiting for thee,
Stand beside thee, every day.'

Lord, and is it Thou, indeed,
Takest pity on my need,
Who nor symbol show nor token
Vouching aught of right in me?
'I, dear soul,' the Master said,
'Come to some through broken bread;
Come to some through message spoken;
Come in pure, free grace to thee.'

———————

JOHN KELLS INGRAM (1823-1907)

Utinam Viderem

'O would,' said holy Bernard, 'I could see
The Church of God as in the days of old!'
So yearns my feebler spirit to behold —
Ah! yet far off — thy Church, Humanity!
As in the coming ages it shall be,
When nations shall be gather'd in thy fold,
In every tongue thy oracles be told,
And millions in thy temples bow the knee.
Then we no more shall spend our wealth of love
Upon imagin'd beings in the skies,
Or waste our thoughts on things beyond our ken;
But flood our hearts with human sympathies,
Content our planet dwelling to improve,
And solace raise, and bless our brother-men.

WILLIAM ALLINGHAM (1824-1889)

from *Blackberries*

Almighty Lord, if day by day
From Thee I further move away,
O let me die tonight, I pray!

Yet no: this pray'r is idle breath.
I understand not life or death,
Nor how man's course continueth.

Swept in a wide and trackless curve,
Though seeming more and more to swerve,
An orbit still it must preserve.

I will not seek to live or die;
Do as Thou wilt, I'll not ask why.
Keep hold of me — content am I.

*   *   *   *

One friendly look, out of the vague and vast!
One certain word to us, O God, at last!
— How should'st thou know, poor child, the look, the word?
Things understood, and not things seen or heard,
Can profit. Many messages thou hast.

*   *   *   *

You may sketch the world of what shape you please,
But the Lord will not alter His lines for these.

*   *   *   *

Adventurous Spirit, trying every road,
You'll find you come to nothing, or to God.

Levavi Oculos

In trouble for my sin, I cried to God;
To the Great God who dwelleth in the deeps.
The deeps return not any voice or sign.

But with my soul I know thee, O Great God
The soul thou gavest kneweth thee, Great God;
And with my soul I sorrow for my sin.

Full sure I am there is no joy in sin,
Joy-scented Peace is trampled under foot
Like a white growing blossom into mud.

Sin is established subtly in the heart
As a disease; like a magician foul
Ruleth the better thoughts against their will.

Only the ways of God can cure the heart,
Purge it of evil: there's no other way
Except to turn with the whole heart to God.

In heavenly sunlight lives no shades of fear;
The soul there, busy or at rest, hath peace;
And music floweth from the various world.

The Power is great and good, and is our God.
There needeth not a word but only these;
Our God is good, our God is great. 'Tis well.

All things are our God's; men's thoughts of things
Are warp'd with evil will and stain'd with sin;
God, and the things of God's, immutable.

Great Master, how I fain would lift myself
Above men's network foolishness, and move
In Thy unfenced, unmeasured warmth and light!

Lo, when I rise a very little way,
The fences, nets, and pitfalls change to lines
Drawn on a map; anon they disappear;

All shows of things are seen as parts of truth;
My soul, if busy or at rest, hath peace,
Hath visions of the House of Perfect Peace.

Mea Culpa

I

At me one night the angry moon,
   Suspended to a rim of cloud,
   Glared through the courses of the wind.
   Suddenly then my spirit bow'd
And shrank into a fearful swoon
   That made me deaf and blind.

II

We sin'd — we sin — is that a dream?
   We wake — there is no voice nor stir;
   Sin and repent from day to day,
   As though some reeking murderer
Should dip his hand in a running stream
   And lightly go his way.

III

Embrace me, friends and wicked men,
   For I am of your crew. Draw back,
   Pure women, children with clear eyes
   Let Scorn confess me on his rack, —

Stretch'd down by force, uplooking then
   Into the solemn skies.

IV

Singly we pass the gloomy gate;
  Some robed in honour, full of peace,
  Who of themselves are not aware,
  Being fed with secret wickedness,
And comforted with lies: my fate
   Moves fast; I shall come there.

V

With all so usual, hour by hour,
  And feeble will so lightly twirl'd
  By every little breeze of sense,
  Lay'st thou to heart this common world?
Lay'st thou to heart the Ruling Power,
   Just, infinite, intense?

VI

Thou wilt not frown, O God. Yet we
  Escape not thy transcendent law;
  It reigns within us and without.
  What earthly vision never saw,
Man's naked soul may suddenly see,
   Dreadful, past thought or doubt.

THOMAS D'ARCY McGEE (1825-1868)

Eternity

Dies irae, dies illa,
Solvet seculum in favilla

I

All men are marshall'd in array,
And order'd for the Judgment Day!
The grave is but a gate whereby
They pass into eternity.

II

More fearful will that hour be
When every wave of every sea
Will find a voice, and all shall cry —
'Behold, behold eternity!'

III

The metals which the mountains hold,
Like tears adown them shall be roll'd;
The blinded earth, the shining sun,
To the dread end will stagger on!

IV

Nought shall endure from pole to pole,
Nought, save th'imperishable soul;
The sea shall pass, the stars decay,
Souls only can survive that day!

V

O God of Justice! God of Love!
Rain down Thy mercies from above,
And make our sinful souls to be
Worthy to dwell for aye with Thee!

VI

Teach us to live our little time,
By Thy delivered law sublime!
Teach us to die, so that we may
Endure, in faith, Thy Judgment Day!

I Will go to the Altar of God
Suggested by the entrance to the Holy Mass

In the night-time I groan'd on my bed,
I felt, O my Father! thy rod;
I felt all thy beauty and truth;
In the morning I rose and I said,
'I will go to the altar of God,
To God, who rejoiceth my youth.'

II

I arose, and knelt under the sign
 Of Him who the wine-press hath trod,
  Where it shone like a ruby, in sooth;
And my soul drank the holocaust wine,
 As I knelt at the altar of God–
  'Of God who rejoiceth my youth.'

III

Despair not, O sorrowing friend!
 Down, down on the stone or the sod;
  To our Father, all mercy and truth;
Cry aloud, 'I repent! I amend!
 I will go to the altar of God,
  To God, who rejoiceth my youth.'

———————————

JOHN TODHUNTER(1839-1916)

The Christ-Child

The Christ-Child came to my bed one night,
 He came in tempest and thunder;
His presence woke me in sweet affright,
 I trembled for joy and wonder;
He bore sedately his Christmas-tree,
 It shone like a silver willow,
His grave child's eyes looked wistfully,
 As he laid a branch on my pillow.

And when he had left me alone, alone,
 And all the house lay sleeping,
I planted it in a nook of my own,
 And watered it with my weeping.
And there it strikes its roots in the earth,
 And opens its leaves to heaven;
And when its blossoms have happy birth
 I shall know my sins forgiven.

———————————

JOHN BOYLE O'REILLY (1844-1890)

Prometheus – Christ

Lashed to the planet, glaring at the sky,
An eagle at his heart – the Pagan Christ!

Why is it, Mystery? O, dumb Darkness, why
Have always men, with loving hearts themselves,
Made devils of their gods?
           The whirling globe
Bears round man's sweating agony of blood,
That Might may ghost above impotent Pain!

Man's soul is dual – he is half a fiend,
And from himself he typifies Almighty.
O, poison-doubt, the answer holds no peace;
Man did not make himself a fiend, but God.

Between them, what? Prometheus stares
Through ether to the lurid eyes of Jove –
Between them, Darkness!

           But the gods are dead –
Ay, Zeus is dead, and all the gods but Doubt,
And Doubt is brother devil to Despair!

What, then, for us? Better Prometheus' fate
Who dared the gods, than insect unbelief –
Better Doubt's fitful flame than abject nothingness!

O, world around us, glory of the spheres!
God speaks in ordered harmony – behold!
Between us and the Darkness, clad in light, –
Between us and the curtain of the Vast, – two Forms,
And each is crowned eternally – and One
Is crowned with flowers and tender leaves and grass,
And smiles benignly; and the other One,
With sadly pitying eyes, is crowned with thorns:
O Nature, and O Christ, for men to love
And seek and live by – Thine the dual reign –
The health and hope and happiness of men!

28

Behold our faith and fruit! –
                    What demon laughs?

Behold our books, our schools, our states,
Where Christ and Nature are the daily word;
Behold our dealings between man and man,
Our laws for home, our treaties for abroad;
Behold our honor, honesty, and freedom,
And, lost, our brotherhood! For we are born
In Christian times and ruled by Christian rules!

Bah! God is mild, or he would strike the world
As men should smite a liar on the mouth.
Shame on the falsehood! Let us tell the truth –
Nor Christ nor Nature rules, but Green and Creed
And Caste and Cant and Craft and Ignorance.
Down to the dust with every decent face,
And whisper there the lies we daily live.
O, God forgive us! Nature never can;
For one is merciful, the other just.

Let us confess: by Nations first – our lives
Are writ in blood and rapine and revenge;
Conquest and pride have motive been and law –
Christ walks with us to hourly crucifixion!

As Men? Would God the better tale were here:
Atom as whole, corruption, shrewdness, self.
Freedom? A juggle –hundreds slave for one, –
That one is free, and boasts, and lo! the shame,
The hundreds at the wheel go boasting too.
Justice? The selfish only can succeed;
Success means power – did Christ mean it so? –
And power must be guarded by the law,
And preachers preach that law must be obeyed,
Ay, even when Right is ironed in the dock,
And Rapine sits in ermine on the bench!
Mercy? Behold it in the reeking slums
That grow like cancers from the palace wall;
Go hear it from the conquered – how their blood
Is weighed in drops, and purchased, blood for gold;
Go ask the toiling tenant why he paid
The landlord's rent and let his children starve;

Go find the thief, whose father was a thief,
And ask what Christian leech has cured his sin?
Honesty? Our law of life is Gain –
We must get gold or be accounted fools;
The lovable, the generous, must be crushed
And substituted by the hard and shrewd.

What is it, Christ, this thing called Christian life,
Where Christ is not, where ninety slave for ten,
And never own a flower save when they steal it,
And never hear a bird save when they cage it?
Is this the freedom of Thy truth? Ah, woe
For those who see a higher, nobler law
Than his, the Crucified, if this be so!

O, man's blind hope – Prometheus, thine the gift –
That bids him live when reason bids him die!
We cling to this, as sailors to a spar –
We see that this is Truth: that men are one,
Nor King nor slave among them save by law.

We see that law is crime, save God's sweet code
That laps the world in freedom: trees and man
And every life around us, days and seasons,
All for their natural order on the planet,
To live their lives, an hour, a hundred years,
Equal, content, and free – nor curse their souls
With trade's malign unrest, with books that breed
Disparity, contempt for those who cannot read;
With cities full of toil and sin and sorrow,
Climbing the devil-builded hill called Progress!

Prometheus, we reject thy gifts for Christ's!
Selfish and hard were thine; but His are sweet –
'Sell what thou hast and give it to the poor!'
Him we must follow to the great Commune,
Reading his book of Nature, growing wise
As planet-men, who own the earth, and pass;
Him we must follow till foul Cant and Caste
Die like disease, and Mankind, freed at last,
Tramples the complex life and laws and limits
That stand between all living things and Freedom!

OSCAR WILDE (1854-1900)

Sonnet
On Hearing the Dies Irae sung in the Sistine Chapel

Nay, Lord, not thus! white lilies in the spring,
    Sad olive-groves, or silver-breasted dove,
    Teach me more clearly of Thy life and love
Than terrors of red flames and thundering.
The empurpled vines dear memories of Thee bring:
    A bird at evening flying to its nest
    Tells me of One who had no place of rest:
I think it is of Thee the sparrows sing.
Come rather on some autumn afternoon,
    When red and brown are burnished on the leaves,
    And the fields echo to the gleaner's song.
Come when the splendid fullness of the moon
    Looks down upon the rows of golden sheaves,
    And reap Thy harvest; we have waited long.

KATHERINE TYNAN (1861-1931)

Sheep and Lambs

All in the April evening,
    April airs were abroad;
The sheep with their little lambs
    Passed me by on the road.

The sheep with their little lambs
    Passed me by, on the road;
All in an April evening,
    I thought on the Lamb of God.

The lambs were weary, and crying
    With a weak, human cry.
I thought on the Lamb of God
    Going meekly to die.

Up in the blue, blue mountain
    Dewy pastures are sweet;
Rest for the little bodies,
    Rest for the little feet.

But for the Lamb of God
   Up on the hill-top green,
Only a Cross of shame,
   Two stark crosses between.

All in the April evening,
   April airs were abroad;
I saw the sheep with their lambs,
   And thought on the Lamb of God.

Mater Dei

She looked to east, she looked to west,
   Her eyes, unfathomable, mild,
That saw both worlds, came home to rest,–
   Home to her own sweet child:
God's golden head was at her breast.

What need to look o'er land and sea?
   What could the winged ships bring to her?
What gold or gems of price might be,
   Ivory or miniver,
Since God Himself lay on her knee?

What could th'intense blue heaven keep
   To draw her eyes and thoughts so high?
All heaven was where her Boy did leap,
   Where her foot quietly
Went rocking the dear God asleep.

The angel folk fared up and down
   A Jacob's ladder hung between
Her quiet chamber and God's Town.
   She saw unawed, serene;
Since God Himself played by her gown.

WILLIAM BUTLER YEATS (1865-1939)

The Ballad of Father Gilligan

The old priest Peter Gilligan
Was weary night and day;
For half his flock were in their beds,
Or under green sods lay.

Once, while he nodded on a chair,
At the moth-hour of eve,
Another poor man sent for him,
And he began to grieve.

'I have no rest, nor joy, nor peace,
For people die and die';
And after cried he, 'God forgive!
My body spake, not I.'

He knelt, and leaning on a chair
He prayed and fell asleep;
And the moth-hour went from the fields,
And stars began to peep.

They slowly into millions grew,
And leaves shook in the wind;
And God covered the world with shade,
And whispered to mankind.

Upon the time of sparrow-chirp
When the moths came once more,
The old priest Peter Gilligan
Stood upright on the floor.

'Mavrone, mavrone! the man has died
While I slept on the chair';
He roused his horse out of its sleep,
And rode with little care.

He rode now as he never rode,
By rocky lane and fen;
The sick man's wife opened the door;
'Father! you come again!'

'And is the poor man dead?' he cried.
'He died an hour ago.'
The old priest Peter Gilligan
In grief swayed to and fro.

'When you were gone, he turned and died
As merry as a bird.'
The old priest Peter Gilligan
He knelt him at that word.

'He who hath made the night of stars
For souls who tire and bleed,
Sent one of His great angels down
To help me in my need.

'He who is wrapped in purple robes,
With planets in His care,
Had pity on the least of things
Asleep upon a chair.'

The Cold Heaven

Suddenly I saw the cold and rook-delighted heaven
That seemed as though ice burned and was but the more ice,
And thereupon imagination and heart were driven
So wild that every casual thought of that and this
Vanished, and left but memories, that should be out of season
With the hot blood of youth, of love crossed long ago;
And I took all the blame out of all sense and reason,
Until I cried and trembled and rocked to and fro,
Riddled with light. Ah! when the ghost begins to quicken,
Confusion of the death-bed over, is it sent
Out naked on the roads, as the books say, and stricken
By the injustice of the skies for punishment?

A Prayer for My Son

Bid a strong ghost stand at the head
That my Michael may sleep sound,
Nor cry, nor turn in the bed
Till his morning meal come round;

And may departing twilight keep
All dread afar till morning's back,
That his mother may not lack
Her fill of sleep.

Bid the ghost have sword in fist:
Some there are, for I avow
Such devilish things exist,
Who have planned his murder, for they know
Of some most haughty deed or thought
That waits upon his future days,
And would through hatred of the bays
Bring that to nought.

Though You can fashion everything
From nothing every day, and teach
The morning stars to sing,
You have lacked articulate speech
To tell Your simplest want, and known,
Wailing upon a woman's knee,
All of that worst ignominy
Of flesh and bone;

And when through all the town there ran
The servants of Your enemy,
A woman and a man,
Unless the Holy Writings lie,
Hurried through the smooth and rough
And through the fertile and waste,
Protecting, till the danger past,
With human love.

Veronica's Napkin

The Heavenly Circuit; Berenice's Hair;
Tent-pole of Eden; the tent's drapery;
Symbolical glory of the earth and air!
The Father and His angelic hierarchy
That made the magnitude and glory there
Stood in the circuit of a needle's eye.

Some found a different pole, and where it stood
A pattern on a napkin dipped in blood.

The Mother of God

The threefold terror of love; a fallen flare
Through the hollow of an ear;
Wings beating about the room;
The terror of all terrors that I bore
The Heavens in my womb.

Had I not found content among the shows
Every common woman knows,
Chimney corner, garden walk,
Or rocky cistern where we tread the clothes
And gather all the talk?

What is this flesh I purchased with my pains,
This fallen star my milk sustains,
This love that makes my heart's blood stop
Or strikes a sudden chill into my bones
And bids my hair stand up?

Vacillation

I

Between extremities
Man runs his course;
A brand, or flaming breath,
Comes to destroy
All those antinomies
Of day and night;
The body calls it death,
The heart remorse.
But if these be right
What is joy?

II

A tree there is that from its topmost bough
Is half all glittering flame and half all green
Abounding foliage moistened with the dew;

36

And half is half and yet is all the scene;
And half and half consume what they renew,
And he that Attis' image hangs between
That starting fury and the blind lush leaf
May know not what he knows, but knows not grief.

III

Get all the gold and silver that you can,
Satisfy ambition, animate
The trivial days and ram them with the sun,
And yet upon these maxims meditate;
All women dote upon an idle man
Although their children need a rich estate;
No man has ever lived that had enough
Of children's gratitude or woman's love.
No longer in Lethean foliage caught
Begin the preparation for your death
And from the fortieth winter by that thought
Test every work of intellect or faith,
And everything that your own hands have wrought,
And call these works extravagance of breath
That are not suited for such men as come
Proud, open-eyed and laughing to the tomb.

IV

My fiftieth year had come and gone,
I sat, a solitary man,
In a crowded London shop,
An open book and empty cup
On the marble table-top.

While on the shop and street I gazed
My body of a sudden blazed;
And twenty minutes more or less
It seemed, so great my happiness
That I was blessèd and could bless.

V

Although the summer sunlight gild
Cloudy leafage of the sky,
Or wintry moonlight sink the field
In storm-scattered intricacy,
I cannot look thereon,
Responsibility so weighs me down.

Things said or done long years ago,
Or things I did not do or say
But thought that I might say or do,
Weigh me down, and not a day
But something is recalled,
My conscience or my vanity appalled.

VI

A rivery field spread out below,
An odour of the new-mown hay
In his nostrils, the great lord of Chou
Cried, casting off the mountain snow,
'Let all things pass away'.

Wheels by milk-white asses drawn
Where Babylon or Nineveh
Rose; some conqueror drew rein
And cried to battle-weary men,
'Let all things pass away'.

From man's blood-sodden heart are sprung
Those branches of the night and day
Where the gaudy moon is hung.
What's the meaning of all song?
'Let all things pass away'.

VII

The Soul. Seek out Reality, leave things that seem.
The Heart. What, be a singer born and lack a theme?
The Soul. Isaiah's coal, what more can man desire?
The Heart. Struck dumb in the simplicity of fire!
The Soul. Look on that fire, salvation walks within.
The Heart. What theme had Homer but original sin?

VIII

Must we part, Von Hügel, though much alike, for we
Accept the miracles of the saints and honour sanctity?
The body of Saint Teresa lies undecayed in tomb,
Bathed in miraculous oil sweet odours from it come,
Healing from its lettered slab. Those self-same hands perchance
Eternalised the body of a modern saint that once
Had scooped out Pharaoh's mummy. I – though heart might find relief
Did I become a Christian man and choose for my belief

What seems most welcome in the tomb – play a predestined part.
Homer is my example and his unchristened heart.
The lion and the honeycomb, what has Scripture said?
So get you gone, Von Hügel, though with blessings on your head.

Ribh Considers Christian Love Insufficient

Why should I seek for love or study it?
It is of God and passes human wit.
I study hatred with great diligence,
For that's a passion in my own control,
A sort of besom that can clear the soul
Of everything that is not mind or sense.

Why do I hate man, woman or event?
That is a light my jealous soul has sent.
From terror and deception freed it can
Discover impurities, can show at last
How soul may walk when all such things are past,
How soul could walk before such things began.

Then my delivered soul herself shall learn
A darker knowledge and in hatred turn
From every thought of God mankind has had.
Thought is a garment and the soul's a bride
That cannot in that trash and tinsel hide:
Hatred of God may bring the soul to God.

At stroke of midnight soul cannot endure
A bodily or mental furniture.
What can she take until her Master give!
Where can she look until He make the show!
What can she know until He bid her know!
How can she live till in her blood He live!

GEORGE WILLIAM RUSSELL (AE) (1867-1935)

A Memory

You remember, dear, together
  Two children, you and I,
Sat once in the autumn weather,
  Watching the autumn sky.

There was some one round us straying
  The whole of the long day through,
Who seemed to say, 'I am playing
  At hide and seek with you.'

And one thing after another
  Was whispered out of the air,
How God was a big, kind brother
  Whose home is in everywhere.

His light like a smile comes glancing
  Through the cool, cool winds as they pass
From the flowers in heaven dancing
  To the stars that shine in the grass.

From the clouds in deep blue wreathing
  And most from the mountains tall,
But God like a wind goes breathing
  A dream of Himself in all.

The heart of the Wise was beating
  Sweet, sweet, in our hearts that day:
And many a thought came fleeting
  And fancies solemn and gay.

We were grave in our way divining
  How childhood was taking wings,
And the wonder world was shining
  With vast eternal things.

The solemn twilight fluttered
  Like the plumes of seraphim,
And we felt what things were uttered
  In the sunset voice of Him.

We lingered long, for dearer
  Than home were the mountain places
Where God from the stars dropt nearer
  Our pale, dreamy faces.

Our very hearts from beating
  We stilled in awed delight,
For spirit and children were meeting
  In the purple, ample light.

Faith

Here where the loves of others close
The vision of my heart begins.
The wisdom that within us grows
In absolution for our sins.

We took forbidden fruit and ate
Far in the garden of His mind.
The ancient prophecies of hate
We proved untrue, for He was kind.

He does not love the bended knees,
The soul made wormlike in His sight,
Within whose heaven are hierarchies
And solar kings and lords of light.

Who come before Him with the pride
The children of the King should bear,
They will not be by Him denied,
His light will make their darkness fair.

To be afar from him is death
Yet all things find their fount in Him:
And nearing to the sunrise breath
Shine jewelled like the seraphim.

―――――――

JOHN MILLINGTON SYNGE (1871-1909)

(The Creed)

My thinking clear, soul powerful, my sight
The wealth of sun, moon, sea, cloud-vesture drains,
The loneliness of heather breathes delight,
I court steep streamlets, withered woods, and lanes.

For my soul I would a world create,
A Christless creed, incredulous, divine,
With Earth's young majesty would yearning mate
The arms of God around my breast intwine.

(In Rebellion)

Thrice cruel fell my fate,
Did I, death tortured, see,
A God, inhuman, great,
Sit weaving woes for me.

So hung as Hell the world,
Death's light with venom stung,
Toward God high taunts I hurled,
With cursing parched my tongue.

JOSEPH CAMPBELL (1879-1944)

When Rooks Fly Homeward

When rooks fly homeward
And shadows fall,
When roses fold
On the hay-yard wall,
When blind moths flutter
By door and tree,
   Then comes the quiet
   Of Christ to me.

When stars look out
On the Children's Path,
And grey mists gather
On carn and rath,
When night is one
With the brooding sea,
   Then comes the quiet
   Of Christ to me.

I am the Mountainy Singer

I am the mountainy singer,
And I would sing of the Christ
Who followed the paths thro' the mountains
To eat at the people's tryst.

He loved the sun-dark people
As the young man loves his bride,
And he moved among their thatches,
And for them he was crucified.

And the people loved him, also,
More than their houses or lands,
For they had known his pity
And felt the touch of his hands.

And they dreamed with him in the mountains,
And they walked with him on the sea,
And they prayed with him in the garden,
And bled with him on the tree.

Not even by longing and dreaming
May they come to him now,
But by the thorns of sorrow
That bruised his kingly brow.

JAMES STEPHENS (1882-1950)

What Thomas Said in a Pub

I saw God! Do you doubt it?
Do you dare to doubt it?
I saw the Almighty Man! His hand
Was resting on a mountain! And
He looked upon the World and all about it:
I saw him plainer than you see me now
– You mustn't doubt it!

He was not satisfied!
His look was all dissatisfied!
His beard swung on a wind, far out of sight
Behind the world's curve! And there was light
Most fearful from His forehead! And He sighed –
– That star went always wrong, and from the start
I was dissatisfied! –

He lifted up His hand!
I say He heaved a dreadful hand
Over the spinning earth! Then I said – Stay,
You must not strike it, God! I'm in the way!
And I will never move from where I stand! –
He said, – Dear child, I feared that you were dead, –
. . . And stayed His hand!

What the Devil said

It was the night-time! God, the Father Good,
Weary of praises, on a sudden stood
Up from His Throne, and leaned upon the sky:
For He had heard a sound; a little cry,
Thin as a whisper, climbing up the Steep.

And so He looked to where the Earth, asleep,
Rocked with the moon: He saw the whirling sea
Swing round the world in surgent energy,
Tangling the moonlight in its netted foam;
And, nearer, saw the white and fretted dome

44

Of the ice-capped pole spin back a larded ray
To whistling stars, bright as a wizard's day.

But these He passed, with eyes intently wide,
Till, closer still, the mountains He espied
Squatting tremendous on the broad-backed Earth,
Each nursing twenty rivers at a birth!
And then, minutely, sought He for the cry
Had climbed the slant of space so hugely high.

He found it in a ditch outside a town:
A tattered hungry woman, crouching down
By a dead babe – So there was naught to do,
For what is done is done! And sad He drew
Back to His Heaven of ivory and gold:
And as He sat, all suddenly there rolled,
From where the woman wept upon the sod,
Satan's deep voice – *O thou unhappy God!*

JOSEPH MARY PLUNKETT (1887-1916)

I See his Blood upon the Rose

I see his blood upon the rose
And in the stars the glory of his eyes,
His body gleams amid eternal snows,
His tears fall from the skies.

I see his face in every flower;
The thunder and the singing of the birds
Are but his voice – and carven by his power
Rocks are his written words.

His pathways by his feet are worn,
His strong heart stirs the ever-beating sea,
His crown of thorns is twined with every thorn,
His cross is every tree.

The Stars Sang in God's Garden

The stars sang in God's garden;
The stars are the birds of God;
The night-time is God's harvest,
Its fruits are the words of God.

God ploughed His fields at morning,
God sowed His seed at noon,
God reaped and gathered in His corn
At the rising of the moon.

The sun rose up at midnight,
The sun rose red as blood,
It showed the Reaper, the dead Christ,
Upon His cross of wood.

For many live that one may die,
And one must die that many live –
The stars are silent in the sky
Lest my poor songs be fugitive.

––––––––––––––

FRANCIS LEDWIDGE (1891-1917)

God's Remembrance

There came a whisper from the night to me
Like music of the sea, a mighty breath
From out the valley's dewy mouth, and Death
Shook his lean bones, and every coloured tree
Wept in the fog of morning. From the town
Of nests among the branches one old crow
With gaps upon his wings flew far away.
And, thinking of the golden summer glow,
I heard a blackbird whistle half his lay
Among the spinning leaves that slanted down.

And I who am a thought of God's now long
Forgotten in His Mind, and desolate
With other dreams long over, as a gate
Singing upon the wind the anvil song,

Sang of the Spring when first He dreamt of me
In that old town all hills and signs that creak: –
And He remembered me as something far
In old imaginations, something weak
With distance, like a little sparkling star
Drowned in the lavender of evening sea.

———————

F R HIGGINS (1896-1941)

Heresy

What peace have I in holy bonds,
From chiselled holiness on stone,
Where croziers, flowering in white bronze,
And fiery minds have finely shown
The grace of God in metal?

So when the quiet shoes my feet
And this hill-pool has cupped the moon,
I'll lie with God and slowly beat
My lonely thought into a tune,
That we may chant together.

Unravelling no gilded prayer,
I'll praise the Scribe, whose burning lines,
On that pure vellum of blue air,
Shoot crimson stars through golden signs
Around the flaming spiral;

And safe beneath those fiery snakes,
His breviary of sleep I'll tell,
Until the shining morning shakes
This calm hill to a laughing bell
And leads the day with singing.

A Vision of Paradise Park
(after the Old Irish)

While waves were glazed with silence
Beneath a shadow's weight,
The still-house on Grass Island
Locked me in sleep last night;

47

And there, while souls from heaven
Came softly through my sleep,
One dressed in blue mist led me
Through fields of meal and mead.

From black lands we rowed over
The sacred river Boyne,
To where saints gamely sported;
There bagpipes cried with joy
When all God's walking beauties
Went by in nun-like robes
Or played on the grass and coolly
Slipped naked from their clothes.

But, O boys, what a glitter!
Some high-born angels lay
Preening their wings in the mirrored
Air of Lady day;
And glitters like them lit the hedgerows
When Lapp-faced cherubs went
Among the robins that echoed
The chinks of Peter's pence.

Nearby on a lake of music
I saw the Paschal sun
Dance when a hearty psalm tune
Was step-danced on a drum;
For all things moved in music –
Even the Tree of Good
And Evil sang like an anvil
As swords clashed round its fruit.

Cut stone rang with the Lord's name,
Brass eagles sang His glees,
The fingered leaves of laurel
Were folded with His peace;
Inks ran to hold His knowledge
While His own scribe adorned
Stags sheltering in a forest
Of their own legs and horns.

There lolled those wrinkled craftsmen,
Whose fingers once unlaced
The knots of thought in granite
From God's own hiding-place;

Ah, now they're all teetotallers,
Finding those Sunday streets
Of heavenly law and order
Policed by parish priests.

And away on the lake's lone islands,
Beside old beehive homes,
Calm waters hold the daylight
Till stars creep towards each door,
Where winds, turned to a dewfall
And beyond to the voice of hills,
Please God in a stiller music
Than fingered wind or strings.

But these winds welded to glory
And these toned as one bell
In Paradise Park – all coldly
Sank from my eyes, until
One angled and arklike abbey
Through a blue mist shone, like a star
That lingered for the lost Magi,
Then quenched on a grey despair.

So alone I stared on the ghostly,
Frozen and foggy air;
Yes, coldly alone till slowly –
And naked as any snail –
A lost soul stood out on the white air;
And on his iceberg throne
I gazed and saw his dead face –
And that face was my own.

Evangelists

Along this bushy lake-side,
While bishops dripped a net
And heeled their boats of bull-hide
Over the green earth,
They told of holy islands,
Where God sang in a bell –
Of icebergs, where Iscariot
Takes holidays from hell.

Yes, they had sought Hy Breasail;
And under pagan air
Their freightage was the gospel,
They drove each sail with prayer;
But tossed from isles of heaven –
Blown by the Evil One –
They read a starry skyline,
Beneath the midnight sun.

Down here they now make heaven –
Closed in from changing floods;
They weave it, while the daylight
Is cobwebbed in old woods;
They carve its four Evangels
As winged and fiery beasts,
That claw the stone of crosses –
That search the minds of priests!

Let scribes leave these delights in
Wise books of skin and horn,
I'll take my spoils of heaven
From hooks of fish and corn,
I'll land the God who gives me
The feast that gilds each net –
The baptism of dew-time
In woods the winds forget!

Star-Gazers

From the grey east,
Through night, noon and the morning,
Into the west
They followed a blue flame;
Like kingfisher's wings
It went as it was leading
These, the wise kings
From lands without a name.

Whitely it stood
Above a moulding townland
And over the wooden
Green dwellings of the poor,

Till with the dewfall
It quietly slid down and
Shone, as a jewel,
On the brow of a door.

There, with no din,
On floorings of cool rushes,
The wise kings went in –
And from an ingle bed
A young woman smiled,
As proudly in her blushes
She breasted a Child
And on a dream He fed.

Down on the floor
These served Him on the knee, when
Each gave of their store's
Untouchable delights –
Gemmed like a seaboard
And scents preserved from Eden –
Gifts the cold sword
Brought through Arabian nights.

So they arose,
But doing so they opened –
Out of a doze –
His eyes from other worlds;
Then O His look held each mind,
Till each saw, through deep darkness,
Upon Hell's dead wind
The white flag was unfurled.

From the green west,
As out of an aurora,
Into the east
These wise kings picked their way;
Close as God's gossips
They went; and now our skylines
Are hailstoned with stars
That tell – ah, who can say?

Pilgrimage

When the far south glittered
Behind the grey beaded plains,
And cloudier ships were bitted
Along the pale waves,
The showery breeze – that plies
A mile from Ara – stood
And took our boat on sand:
There by dim wells the women tied
A wish on thorn, while rainfall
Was quiet as the turning of books
In the holy schools at dawn.

Grey holdings of rain
Had grown less with the fields,
As we came to that blessed place
Where hail and honey meet.
O Clonmacnoise was crossed
With light: those cloistered scholars,
Whose knowledge of the gospel
Is cast as metal in pure voices,
Were all rejoicing daily,
And cunning hands with cold and jewels
Brought chalices to flame.

Loud above the grassland,
In Cashel of the towers,
We heard with the yellow candles
The chanting of the hours,
White clergy saying High Mass,
A fasting crowd at prayer,
A choir that sang before them:
And in stained glass the holy day
Was sainted as we passed
Beyond that chancel where the dragons
Are carved upon the arch.

Treasured with chasuble,
Sun-braided, rich cloak'd wine-cup,
We saw, there, iron handbells,

Great annals in the shrine
A high-king bore to battle:
Where, from the branch of Adam,
The noble forms of language –
Brighter than green or blue enamels
Burned in white bronze – embodied
The wings and fiery animals
Which veil the chair of God.

Beyond a rocky townland
And that last tower where ocean
Is dim as haze, a sound
Of wild confession rose:
Black congregations moved
Around the booths of prayer
To hear a saint reprove them;
And from his boat he raised a blessing
To souls that had come down
The holy mountain of the west
Or wailed still in the cloud.

Light in the tide of Shannon
May ride at anchor half
The day and, high in spar-top
Or leather sails of their craft,
Wine merchants will have sleep;
But on a barren isle,
Where Paradise is praised
At daycome, smaller than the sea-gulls,
We heard white Culdees pray
Until our hollow ship was kneeling
Over the longer waves.

Night and Morning

I know the injured pride of sleep,
The strippers at the mocking-post,
The insult in the house of Caesar
And every moment that can hold
In brief the miserable act
Of centuries. Thought can but share

Belief – and the tormented soul,
Changing confession to despair,
Must wear a borrowed robe.

Morning has moved the dreadful candle,
Appointed shadows cross the nave;
Unlocked by the secular hand,
The very elements remain
Appearances upon the altar.
Adoring priest has turned his back
Of gold upon the congregation.
All saints have had their day at last,
But thought still lives in pain.

How many councils and decrees
Have perished in the simple prayer
That gave obedience to the knee;
Trampling of rostrum, feathering
Of pens at cock-rise, sum of reason
To elevate a common soul:
Forgotten as the minds that bled
For us, the miracle that raised
A language from the dead.

O when all Europe was astir
With echo of learned controversy,
The voice of logic led the choir.
Such quality was in all being,
The forks of heaven and this earth
Had met, town-walled, in mortal view
And in the pride that we ignore,
The holy rage of argument,
God was made man once more.

Tenebrae

This is the hour that we must mourn
With tallows on the black triangle,
Night has a napkin deep in fold
To keep the cup; yet who dare pray
If all in reason should be lost,
The agony of man betrayed
At every station of the cross?

O when the forehead is too young,
Those centuries of mortal anguish,
Dabbed by a consecrated thumb
That crumbles into dust, will bring
Despair with all that we can know;
And there is nothing left to sing,
Remembering our innocence.

I hammer on that common door,
Too frantic in my superstition,
Transfix with nails that I have broken,
The angry notice of the mind,
Close as the thought that suffers him,
The habit every man in time
Must wear beneath his ironed shirt.

An open mind disturbs the soul,
And in disdain I turn my back
Upon the sun that makes a show
Of half the world, yet still deny
The pain that lives within the past,
The flame sinking upon the spike,
Darkness that man must dread at last.

Martha Blake

Before the day is everywhere
And the timid warmth of sleep
Is delicate on limb, she dares
The silence of the street
Until the double bells are thrown back
For Mass and echoes bound
In the chapel yard, O then her soul
Makes bold in the arms of sound.

But in the shadow of the nave
Her well-taught knees are humble,
She does not see through any saint
That stands in the sun
With veins of lead, with painful crown;
She waits that dreaded coming,
When all the congregation bows
And none may look up.

The word is said, the Word sent down,
The miracle is done
Beneath those hands that have been rounded
Over the embodied cup,
And with a few, she leaves her place
Kept by an east-filled window
And kneels at the communion rail
Starching beneath her chin.

She trembles for the Son of Man,
While the priest is murmuring
What she can scarcely tell, her heart
Is making such a stir;
But when he picks a particle
And she puts out her tongue,
That joy is the glittering of candles
And benediction sung.

Her soul is lying in the Presence
Until her senses, one
By one, desiring to attend her,
Come as for feast and run
So fast to share the sacrament,
Her mouth must mother them:
'Sweet tooth grow wise, lip, gum be gentle,
I touch a purple hem.'

Afflicted by that love she turns
To multiply her praise,
Goes over all the foolish words
And finds they are the same;
But now she feels within her breast
Such calm that she is silent,
For soul can never be immodest
Where body may not listen.

On a holy day of obligation
I saw her first in prayer,
But mortal eye had been too late
For all that thought could dare.
The flame in heart is never grieved
That pride and intellect
Were cast below, when God revealed
A heaven for this earth.

So to begin the common day
She needs a miracle,
Knowing the safety of angels
That see her home again,
Yet ignorant of all the rest,
The hidden grace that people
Hurrying to business
Look after in the street.

The Straying Student

On a holy day when sails were blowing southward,
A bishop sang the Mass at Inishmore,
Men took one side, their wives were on the other
But I heard the woman coming from the shore:
And wild in despair my parents cried aloud
For they saw the vision draw me to the doorway.

Long had she lived in Rome when Popes were bad,
The wealth of every age she makes her own,
Yet smiled on me in eager admiration,
And for a summer taught me all I know,
Banishing shame with her great laugh that rang
As if a pillar caught it back alone.

I learned the prouder counsel of her throat,
My mind was growing bold as light in Greece;
And when in sleep her stirring limbs were shown,
I blessed the noonday rock that knew no tree:
And for an hour the mountain was her throne
Although her eyes were bright with mockery.

They say I was sent back from Salamanca
And failed in logic, but I wrote her praise
Nine times upon a college wall in France.
She laid her hand at darkfall on my page
That I might read the heavens in a glance
And I knew every star the Moors have named.

Awake or in my sleep, I have no peace now,
Before the ball is struck, my breath has gone,
And yet I tremble lest she may deceive me

And leave me in this land, where every woman's son
Must carry his own coffin and believe,
In dread, all that the clergy teach the young.

The Envy of Poor Lovers

Pity poor lovers who may not do what they please
With their kisses under a hedge, before a raindrop
Unhouse it; and astir from wretched centuries,
Bramble and briar remind them of the saints.

Her envy is the curtain seen at night-time,
Happy position that could change her name.
His envy – clasp of the married whose thoughts can be alike,
Whose nature flows without the blame or shame.

Lying in the grass as if it were a sin
To move, they hold each other's breath, tremble,
Ready to share that ancient dread – kisses begin
Again – of Ireland keeping company with them.

Think, children, of institutions mured above
Your ignorance, where every look is veiled,
State-paid to snatch away the folly of poor lovers
For whom, it seems, the sacraments have failed.

Ancient Lights

When all of us wore smaller shoes
And knew the next world better than
The knots we broke, I used to hurry
On missions of my own to Capel
Street, Bolton Street and Granby Row
To see what man has made. But darkness
Was roomed with fears. Sleep, stripped by woes
I had been taught, beat door, leaped landing,
Lied down the bannisters of naught.

Being sent to penance, come Saturday,
I shuffled slower than my sins should,
My fears were candle-spiked at side-shrines,

58

Rays lengthened them in stained-glass. Confided
To night again, my grief bowed down.
Heard hand on shutter-knob. Did I
Take pleasure, when alone – how much –
In a bad thought, immodest look
Or worse, unnecessary touch?

Closeted in the confessional
I put on flesh, so many years
Were added to my own, attempted
In vain to keep Dominican
As much in the dark as I was, mixing
Whispered replies with the low words;
Then shuddered past the crucifix,
The feet so hammered, daubed-on blood-drip,
Black with lip-scrimmage of the damned.

Once as I crept from the church-steps,
Beside myself, the air opened
On purpose. Nature read in a flutter
An evening lesson above my head.
Atwirl beyond the leadings, corbels,
A cage-bird came among sparrows
(The moral inescapable)
Plucked, roof-mired, all in mad bits. O
The pizzicato of its wires!

Goodness of air can be proverbial:
That day, by the kerb at Rutland Square,
A bronze bird fabled out of trees,
Mailing the spearheads of the railings,
Sparrow at nails. I hailed the skies
To save the tiny dropper, found
Appetite gone. A child of clay
Had blustered it away. Pity
Could raise some littleness from dust.

What Sunday clothes can change us now
Or humble orders in black and white?
Stinking with centuries the act
Of thought. So think, man, as Augustine
Did, dread the ink-bespattered ex-monk,
And keep your name. No, let me abandon

59

Night's jakes. Self-persecuted of late
Among the hatreds of rent Europe,
Poetry burns at a different stake.

Still, still I remember aweful downpour
Cabbing Mountjoy Street, spun loneliness
Veiling almost the Protestant church,
Two backyards from my very home,
I dared to shelter at locked door.
There, walled by heresy, my fears
Were solved. I had absolved myself:
Feast-day effulgence, as though I gained
For life a plenary indulgence.

The sun came out, new smoke flew up,
The gutters of the Black Church rang
With services. Waste water mocked
The ballcocks: down-pipes sparrowing,
And all around the spires of Dublin
Such swallowing in the air, such cowling
To keep high offices pure: I heard
From shore to shore, the iron gratings
Take half our heavens with a roar.

St Christopher

Child that his strength upbore,
Knotted as tree-trunks in the spate,
Became a giant, whose weight
Unearthed the river from shore
Till saint's bones were a-crack.
Fabulist, can an ill state
Like ours, carry so great
A Church upon its back?

Martha Blake at Fifty-One

Early, each morning, Martha Blake
  Walked, angeling the road,
To Mass in the Church of the Three Patrons.
  Sanctuary lamp glowed

And the clerk halo'ed the candles
  On the High Altar. She knelt
Illumined. In gold-hemmed alb,
  The priest intoned. Wax melted.

Waiting for daily Communion, bowed head
  At rail, she hears a murmur.
Latin is near. In a sweet cloud
  That cherub'd, all occurred.
The voice went by. To her pure thought,
  Body was a distress
And soul, a sigh. Behind her denture,
  Love lay, a helplessness.

Then, slowly walking after Mass
  Down Rathgar Road, she took out
Her Yale key, put a match to gas-ring,
  Half filled a saucepan, cooked
A fresh egg lightly, with tea, brown bread.
  Soon, taking off her blouse
And skirt, she rested, pressing the Crown
  Of thorns until she drowsed.

In her black hat, stockings, she passed
  Nylons to a nearby shop
And purchased daily, with downcast eyes,
  Fillet of steak or a chop,
She simmered it on a low heat,
  Having a poor appetite,
Yet never for an hour felt better
  From dilation, tightness.

She suffered from dropped stomach, heartburn
  Scalding, water-brash
And when she brought her wind up, turning
  Red with the weight of mashed
Potato, mint could not relieve her.
  In vain her many belches,
For all below was swelling, heaving
  Wamble, gurgle, squelch.

She lay on the sofa with legs up,
  A decade on her lip,
At four o'clock, taking a cup
  Of lukewarm water, sip

61

By sip, but still her daily food
  Repeated and the bile
Tormented her. In a blue hood,
  The Virgin sadly smiled.

When she looked up, the Saviour showed
  His Heart, daggered with flame
And, from the mantle-shelf, St Joseph
  Bent, disapproving. Vainly
She prayed, for in the whatnot corner
  The new Pope was frowning. Night
And day, dull pain, as in her corns,
  Recounted every bite.

She thought of St Teresa, floating
  On motes of a sunbeam,
Carmelite with scatterful robes,
  Surrounded by demons,
Some black boys in their skin. She gaped
  At Hell: a muddy passage
That led to nothing, queer in shape,
  A cupboard closely fastened.

Sometimes, the walls of the parlour
  Would fade away. No plod
Of feet, rattle of van, in Garville
  Road. Soul now gone abroad
Where saints, like medieval serfs,
  Had laboured. Great sun-flower shone.
Our Lady's Chapel was borne by seraphs,
  Three leagues beyond Ancona.

High towns of Italy, the plain
  Of France, were known to Martha
As she read in a holy book. The sky-blaze
  Nooned at Padua,
Marble grotto of Bernadette.
  Rose-scatterers. New saints
In tropical Africa where the tsetse
  Fly probes, the forest taints.

Teresa had heard the Lutherans
  Howling on the red-hot spit,
And grill, men who had searched for truth
  Alone in Holy Writ.

So Martha, fearful of flame lashing
  Those heretics each instant
Never dealt in the haberdashery
  Shop, owned by two Protestants.

In ambush of night, an angel wounded
  The Spaniard to the heart
With iron tip on fire. Swooning
  With pain and bliss as a dart
Moved up and down within her bowels
  Quicker, quicker, each cell
Sweating as if rubbed up with towels,
  Her spirit rose and fell.

St John of the Cross, her friend, in prison
  Awaits the bridal night,
Paler than lilies, his wizened skin
  Flowers. In fifths of flight,
Senses beyond seraphic thought,
  In that divinest clasp,
Enfolding of kisses that cauterise,
  Yield to the soul-spasm.

Cunning in body and come to hate
  All this and stirred by mischief
Haled Martha from heaven. Heart palpitates
  And terror in her stiffens,
Heart misses one beat, two. . . flutters . . . stops.
  Her ears are full of sound,
Half fainting, she stares at the grandfather clock
  As if it were overwound.

The fit had come. Ill-natured flesh
  Despised her soul. No bending
Could ease rib. Around her heart, pressure
  Of wind grew worse. Again,
Again, armchaired without relief,
  She eructated, phlegm
In mouth, forgot the woe, the grief,
  Foretold at Bethlehem.

Tired of the same faces, side-altars,
  She went to the Carmelite Church,
At Johnson's Court, confessed her faults,
  There, once a week, purchased

63

Tea, butter in Chatham St. The pond
  In St Stephen's Green was grand,
She watched the seagulls, ducks, black swan,
  Went home by the 15 tram.

Her beads in hand, Martha became
  A member of the Third Order,
Saved from long purgatorial pain,
  Brown habit and white cord
Her own when cerges had been lit
  Around her coffin. She got
Ninety-five pounds on loan for her bit
  Of clay in the common plot.

Often she thought of a quiet sick-ward,
  Nuns, with delicious ways,
Consoling the miserable: quick
  Tea, toast on trays. Wishing
To rid themselves of her, kind neighbours
  Sent for the ambulance,
Before her brother and sister could hurry
  To help her. Big gate clanged.

No medical examination
  For the new patient. Doctor
Had gone to Cork on holidays.
  Telephone sprang. Hall-clock
Proclaimed the quarters. Clatter of heels
  On tiles. Corridor, ward.
A-whirr with the electric cleaner,
  The creak of window cord.

She could not sleep at night. Feeble
  And old, two women raved
And cried to God. She held her beads.
  O how could she be saved?
The hospital and this and that rule.
  Day-chill unshuttered. Nun, with
Thermometer in reticule,
  Went by. The women mumbled.

Mother Superior believed
  That she was obstinate, self-willed.
Sisters ignored her, hands-in-sleeves,
  Beside a pantry shelf

64

Of counting pillow-case, soiled sheet.
   They gave her purgatives.
Soul-less, she tottered to the toilet.
   Only her body lived.

Wasted by colitis, refused
   The daily sacrament
By regulation, forbidden use
   Of bed-pan, when meals were sent up,
Behind a screen, she lay, shivering,
   Unable to eat. The soup
Was greasy, mutton, beef or liver,
   Cold. Kitchen has no scruples.

The nuns had let the field in front
   As an Amusement Park,
Merry-go-round, a noisy month, all
   Heltering-skeltering at darkfall,
Mechanical music, dipper, hold-tights,
   Rifle-crack, crash of dodgems.
The ward, godless with shadow, lights,
   How could she pray to God?

Unpitied, wasting with diarrhoea
   And the constant strain,
Poor Child of Mary with one idea,
   She ruptured a small vein,
Bled inwardly to jazz. No priest
   Came. She had been anointed
Two days before, yet knew no peace:
   Her last breath, disappointed.

PATRICK KAVANAGH (1904-1967)

To A Blackbird

O pagan poet you
And I are one
In this – we lose our god
At set of sun.

And we are kindred when
The hill wind shakes
Sweet song like blossoms on
The calm green lakes.

We dream while Earth's sad children
Go slowly by,
Pleading for our conversion
With the Most High.

To a Child

Child do not go
Into the dark places of soul,
For there the grey wolves whine,
The lean grey wolves.

I have been down
Among the unholy ones who tear
Beauty's white robe and clothe her
In rags of prayer.

Child there is light somewhere
Under a star,
Sometime it will be for you
A window that looks
Inward to God.

Beyond the Headlines

When I saw the wild geese flying
In fair formation to their bases in Inchicore
And I knew that these wings would outwear the wings of war
And a man's simple thoughts outlive the day's loud lying
Don't fear, don't fear, I said to my soul.
The Bedlam of Time is an empty bucket rattled,
'Tis you who will say in the end who best battles.
Only they who fly home to God have flown at all.

from
The Great Hunger

IV

April, and no one able to calculate
How far is it to harvest? They put down
The seeds blindly with sensuous groping fingers,
And sensual sleep dreams subtly underground.
To-morrow is Wednesday – who cares?
'Remember Eileen Farrelly? I was thinking
A man might do a damned sight worse...' That voice is blown
Through a hole in a garden wall –
And who was Eileen now cannot be known.

The cattle are out on grass,
The corn is coming up evenly.
The farm folk are hurrying to catch Mass:
Christ will meet them at the end of the world, the slow and speedier.
But the fields say: only Time can bless.

Maguire knelt beside a pillar where he could spit
Without being seen. He turned an old prayer round:
'Jesus, Mary and Joseph pray for us
Now and at the Hour.' Heaven dazzled death,
'Wonder should I cross-plough that turnip-ground.'
The tension broke. The congregation lifted its head
As one man and coughed in unison.
Five hundred hearts were hungry for life –
Who lives in Christ shall never die the death.
And the candle-lit Altar and the flowers
And the pregnant Tabernacle lifted a moment to Prophecy
Out of the clayey hours.
Maguire sprinkled his face with holy water
As the congregation stood up for the Last Gospel.
He rubbed the dust off his kness with his palm, and then
Coughed the prayer phlegm up from his throat and sighed: Amen.

Once one day in June when he was walking
Among his cattle in the Yellow Meadow
He met a girl carrying a basket –
And he was then a young and heated fellow.
To earnest, too earnest! He rushed beyond the thing
To the unreal. And he saw Sin

Written in letters larger than John Bunyan dreamt of.
For the strangled impulse there is no redemption.
And that girl was gone and he was counting
The dangers in the fields where love ranted
He was helpless. He saw cattle
And stroked their flanks in lieu of wife to handle.
He would have changed the circle if he could,
The circle that was the grass track where he ran.
Twenty times a day he ran round the field
And still there was no winning-post where the runner is cheered home.
Desperately he broke the tune,
But however he tried always the same melody crept up from the
  background,
The dragging step of a ploughman going home through the guttery
Headlands under an April-watery moon.
Religion, the fields and the fear of the Lord
And Ignorance giving him the coward's blow,
He dare not rise to pluck the fantasies
From the fruited Tree of Life. He bowed his head
And saw a wet weed twined about his toe.

VI

Health and wealth and love he too dreamed of in May
As he sat on the railway slope and watched the children of the place
Picking up a primrose here and a daisy there –
They were picking up life's truth singly. But he dreamt of the
  Absolute envased bouquet –
All or nothing. And it was nothing. For God is not all
In one place, complete
Till Hope comes in and takes it on his shoulder –
O Christ, that is what you have done for us:
In a crumb of bread the whole mystery is.

He read the symbol too sharply and turned
From the five simple doors of sense
To the door whose combination lock has puzzled
Philosopher and priest and common dunce.
Men build their heavens as they build their circles
Of friends. God is in the bits and pieces of Everyday –
A kiss here and a laugh again, and sometimes tears,
A pearl necklace round the neck of poverty.

He sat on the railway slope and watched the evening,
Too beautifully perfect to use,
And his three wishes were three stones too sharp to sit on,
Too hard to carve. Three frozen idols of a speechless muse.

VII

'Now go to Mass and pray and confess your sins
And you'll have luck,' his mother said.
He listened to the lie that is a woman's screen
Around a conscience when soft thighs are spread.
And all the while she was setting up the lie
She trusted in Nature that never deceives.
But her son took it as literal truth.
Religion's walls expand to the push of nature. Morality yields
To sense – but not in little tillage fields.

Life went on like that. One summer morning
Again through a hay-field on her way to the shop –
The grass was wet and over-leaned the path –
And Agnes held her skirts sensationally up,
And not because the grass was wet either.
A man was watching her, Patrick Maguire.
She was in love with passion and its weakness
And the wet grass could never cool the fire
That radiated from her unwanted womb
In that country, in that metaphysical land
Where flesh was a thought more spiritual than music
Among the stars – out of reach of the peasant's hand.

Ah, but the priest was one of the people too –
A farmer's son – and surely he knew
The needs of a brother and sister.
Religion could not be a counter-irritant like a blister,
But the certain standard measured and known
By which man might re-make his soul though all walls were down
And all earth's pedestalled gods thrown.

XIV

Maguire is not afraid of death, the Church will light him a candle
To see his way through the vaults and he'll understand the
Quality of the clay that dribbles over his coffin.

He'll know the names of the roots that climb down to tickle his feet.
And he will feel no different than when he walked through Donaghmoyne.
If he stretches out a hand – a wet clod,
If he opens his nostrils – a dungy smell;
If he opens his eyes once in a million years –
Through a crack in the crust of the earth he may see a face nodding in
Or a woman's legs. Shut them again for that sight is sin.

He will hardly remember that life happened to him –
Something was brighter a moment. Somebody sang in the distance.
A procession passed down a mesmerised street.
He remembers names like Easter and Christmas
By the colour his fields were.
Maybe he will be born again, a bird of an angel's conceit

To sing the gospel of life
To a music as flightily tangent
As a tune on an oboe.
And the serious look of the fields will have changed to the leer of a
    hobo
Swaggering celestially home to his three wishes granted.
Will that be? will that be?
Or is the earth right that laughs haw-haw
And does not believe
In an unearthly law.
The earth that says:
Patrick Maguire, the old peasant, can neither be damned nor glorified:
The graveyard in which he will lie will be just a deep-drilled potato-
    field
Where the seed gets no chance to come through
To the face of the sun.
The tongue in his mouth is the root of a yew.
Silence, silence. The story is done.
He stands in the doorway of his house
A ragged sculpture of the wind,
October creaks the rotted mattress,
The bedposts fall. No hope. No lust.
The hungry fiend
Screams the apocalypse of clay
In every corner of this land.

Father Mat

In a meadow
Beside the chapel three boys were playing football.
At the forge door an old man was leaning
Viewing a hunter-hoe. A man could hear
If he listened to the breeze the fall of wings –
How wistfully the sin-birds come home!

It was Confession Saturday, the first
Saturday in May; the May Devotions
Were spread like leaves to quieten
The excited armies of conscience.
The knife of penance fell so like a blade
Of grass that no one was afraid.

Father Mat came slowly walking, stopping to
Stare through gaps at ancient Ireland sweeping
In again with all its unbaptised beauty:
The calm evening,
The whitethorn blossoms,
The smell from ditches that were not Christian,
The dancer that dances in the hearts of men cried:

Look! I have shown this to you before –
The rags of living surprised
The joy in things you cannot forget.

His heavy hat was square upon his head,
Like a Christian Brother's;
His eyes were an old man's watery eyes,

Out of his flat nose grew spiky hairs.
He was a part of the place,
Natural as a round stone in a grass field;
He could walk through a cattle fair
And the people would only notice his odd spirit there.

His curate passed on a bicycle –
He had the haughty, intellectual look
Of the man who never reads in brook or book;

A man designed
To wear a mitre,
To sit on committees –
For will grows strongest in the emptiest mind.

The old priest saw him pass
And, seeing, saw
Himself a mediaeval ghost.
Ahead of him went Power,
One who was not afraid when the sun opened a flower,
Who was never astonished
At a stick carried down a stream
Or at the undying difference in the corner of a field.

II

The Holy Ghost descends
At random like the muse
On wise man and fool,
And why should poet in the twilight choose?

Within the dim chapel was the grey
Mumble of prayer
To the Queen of May –
The Virgin Mary with the schoolgirl air.

Two guttering candles on a brass shrine
Raised upon the wall
Monsters of despair
To terrify deep into the soul

Through the open door the hum of rosaries
Came out and blended with the homing bees.
                                    The trees
Heard nothing stranger than the rain or the wind
Or the birds –
But deep in their roots they knew a seed had sinned.

In the graveyard a goat was nibbling at a yew,
The cobbler's chickens with anxious looks
Were straggling home through nettles, over graves.
A young girl down a hill was driving cows
To a corner at the gable-end of a roofless house.

Cows were milked earlier,
The supper hurried,
Hens shut in,
Horses unyoked,
And three men shaving before the same mirror.

III

The trip of iron tips on tile
Hesitated up the middle aisle,
Heads that were bowed glanced up to see
Who could this last arrival be.

Murmur of women's voices from the porch,
Memories of relations in the graveyard
On the stem
Of memory imaginations blossom.

           In the dim
Corners in the side seats faces gather,
Lit up now and then by a guttering candle
And the ghost of day at the window.
A secret lover is saying

Three Hail Marys that she who knows
The ways of women will bring
Cathleen O'Hara (he names her) home to him.
Ironic fate! Cathleen herself is saying
Three Hail Marys to her who knows
The ways of men to bring
Somebody else home to her –
'O may he love me',
What is the Virgin Mary now to do?

IV

      From a confessional
The voice of Father Mat's absolving
Rises and falls like a briar in the breeze.
As the sins pour in the old priest is thinking
His fields of fresh grass, his horses, his cows,
His earth into the fires of Purgatory.
It cools his mind.
'They confess to the fields,' he mused,
'They confess to the fields and the air and the sky,'

And forgiveness was the soft grass of his meadow by the river;
His thoughts were walking through it now.

His human lips talked on:
'My son,
Only the poor in spirit shall wear the crown;
Those down
Can creep in the low door
On to Heaven's floor.'

The Tempter had another answer ready:
'Ah lad, upon the road of life
'Tis best to dance with Chance's wife
And let the rains that come in time
Erase the footprints of the crime.'

The dancer that dances in the hearts of men
Tempted him again:
'Look! I have shown you this before;
From this mountain-top I have tempted Christ
With what you see now
Of beauty – all that's music, poetry, art
In things you can touch every day.
I broke away
And rule all dominions that are rare;
I took with me all the answers to every prayer
That young men and girls pray for: love, happiness, riches –'
O Tempter! O Tempter!

V

As Father Mat walked home
Venus was in the western sky
And there were voices in the hedges;
'God the Gay, is not the Wise.'

'Take your choice, take your choice,'
Called the breeze through the bridge's eye.
'The domestic Virgin and Her Child
Or Venus with her ecstasy.'

MONK GIBBON (1896-1987)

The Ballad of the
Crazy Cowherd

Yesterday I saw
The good Jesus come
Straight from lofty heaven
On his way to Rome,
Hotfoot to receive
From the Church, his Bride,
Mankind's hidden heart
Wholly sanctified.

Ah, what kindness shone
From that brow divine
Piercing like a shaft,
Sun-shot into mine.
Kingcups sprang to birth
As his feet did pass,
Leaving tracks of gold
In the marshy grass.

Soon he left the meadow,
Swift he crossed the stream,
Straight he took the headland
Where the white waves gleam.
Then I ran to stop him,
Him, the Lord and King,
Crying, 'Wait, Lord Jesus,
Wait – there is one thing!'

There he turned and halted,
Small birds swept the air,
Not by hawk made angry,
But by Him made fair.
All along the hedges –
Flakes of fragrant snow –
Hawthorn spilt its sweetness,
'Master, do not go!'

'What perturbs you?' Slowly
Shame came over me,
I who strove to hold him
From the wine-dark sea.
Till at last, that silence
Cutting like a sword,
I in anguish murmured
'Nothing – nothing, Lord.'

'Nothing? Why for nothing
Breathless do you run?
Speak right out, my servant,
Speak your mind, my, son.'
Then I spoke out trembling,
'Lord, you do not know,
Even Peter's successor
Would not want you now.

Even Rome's streets witness
To man's present shame,
Filled with fruit of hatred
Filled with blind and lame,
Filled with limbs grown rotten
Filled with souls whose sores
Cry aloud the horror
Of unholy wars.'

'Is this all, my servant,
All they offer me?'
'Yes, Lord, all at present.
Read the papers, see.
Men are proud and fearful,
Women bitter, sad;
Lord, turn back to heaven
Till times be less bad.'

Then – oh holy angels
Shield my soul – I saw
Him, whose soul is sweetness,
Him, whose word is law
To high heaven, weeping;
Tears of shame ran down,
Tears of blood that falling
Spattered this poor clown

And he cried, 'How often
Had I gathered thee,
Men, my darlings, under
Wings of charity;
As the hen at evening
On the earthen floor
Calls her brood beneath her
By the cottage door.'

Then the Lord turned backward
And he made his way
Once more through the meadow,
Once more up the brae;
As moon's shade at midday
Makes birds sudden still,
So that slow departure
Silenced all the hill,

And I called 'Sweet Jesus,
Though earth should not see
Thee again till Judgment
Blame it, Lord, on me.
Lord, on my head be it
That you did not find
What black-hearted business
Men have still in mind.'

EWART MILNE (1903-1984)

The Bride of Christ

If you want a story of love fulfilled
And not a story of love frustrated
If you want a song of love in bloom
And not the sound of love denigrated
If you want voluptuous kisses and sighs
The lover's rapture the virgin's cries
And not the slow freezing of blood and genitals

Go then and seek them under different skies
For this is Ireland whose song is holy holy holy

This is the land of great Brigid the nun
Whose face is veiled and who lies alone
Untouched until her Lord shall come
Whose bride she is and His chosen one
On the further side of the tomb tomb tomb.

Twilight of an Idol

Build me a Church in the Human loins,
A Tower in the Human head,
A fusion build of the Human heart
With four Walls of its chambers red,
Then man shall serve me and still believe he is free
And both be satisfied,
Said the God of the World, the Jealous God.

They built Him a Church in the Human loins
That on the lovely genitals stood,
They built Him a Tower in the Human mind
And within from without enclosed;
The Human heart they cleft apart
And divided in two and four,
And grey were its walls where the sun had outshone.

To His Servants again spoke the Jealous God
And this command He gave:
To make Him a Harp of man's high breastbone
That his unending lament might be turned
And measured there with the murmuring joy
Of the babe new-born into swaddling bands,
And its shadow cast on the growing boy.

Then His Servants took man and nailed him down
While ever he claimed his rest,
They opened him up and placed a Harp
In the cave of his gaping breast;
Then the Harp they wired to his animal loins,
To the Tower of his mind, to his prisoned heart,
And the wires they crossed and crossed again
Until none could tell them apart.

The Church in his loins sang loud of sin,
His heart struck a hollow gong,
From the Tower of his mind an armed man spoke
And urged him to strife and wrong;
Until at length he rose in wrath
To rebel against Church, break prison and Tower
And would have plucked the Harp from his breast
But that it sang his freedom hour . . .

And sang the death of the Jealous God
Outstretched beneath a Tree,
Where he had fallen from his perch on a cloud
At that bitter cry of liberty.
And still there sounds the Harp today,
And still from loins and heart come moan,
For freedom is of the senses five, and not of the head alone.

PADRAIC FALLON (1905-1974)

Holy Well

In the annals saints
Sit in holy wells, talk freely
To grim hermits, heal
Who ails, the foot-holy
Pilgrims who walk in wishes.

The dumb speak, the cripple
Walks, the blind
Find the dazzling world of the mind
In new pigments. Here
The ways of God seem wayward but very dear.

Speak the word, Saint,
In your welling mineral
That world in a bright and single jet
Go up, and inside it, lit up,
God my space and my material.

The Christmas Vigil

Wherever else the real miracle
Was happening, with climates curtsying
To the small holy city, out here
On the west periphery
Our Galway weather hadn't nodded east.

Elsewhere the nub
And circles of rejoicing heaven, stars high and low
Lifting to the skyline
The figures of donkey, man and virgin
Moving towards Bethlehem.

So, on the old cart
Bumping on the road by Lopdells, today
Had not arrived, the trees
With aboriginal arms still making
Yesterday's rain

From the day's soft grey substance; no
New magnitude in the stone
Fields, no distances starting to flow
Into rainbows; there was only this
Same old world with yesterday's leftovers.

All the way to Mountbawn, with
Bullocks in a horned frieze staring
Egyptian from the roughmasoned gateways, ours
Storming the cart as we appeared;
We tossed them their turnips and went wheeling

Over the usual earth. Obviously
Christmas had not come to the brutes on this
Waterhaunted ledge of the Atlantic. It
Was quiet in the lambing paddocks, the ewes
Waiting at the troughs

In sops of gold straw for the broken oats;
And we dished it out, we two
Shepherds of sorts though no sky would open
For Nicholas Moran pipe in mouth now
And quite happy in his wingless span

Of Galway clay. Me too, for miracles belong
Over the ultimate horizon; nothing here
Has learned the rudiments,
No beast of ours
Drizzling over his fat roots will turn celestial,

Unlike the Bible ox
In the crib under the organ gallery, where
With a star strung like a kite above
And the new lunation in its eye,
The beast lights up with human love.

But this is the mystery welling
Up from some inner world in a sort
Of perennial heartbeat. All day the glow of it
Fills the back of my mind; but I won't look;
Not yet

Being simply afraid of what could happen.
I like things as they are,
World as it is, the wonder just round the corner;
And if at midnight
All the clocks in the world meet to chime

Over the world's newest child, this
Will be the more spacious for happening in my sleep
Where ends can meet in peace
When the great harps sweep out upon the pediments
And the wren waken with a tiny cheep.

Virgin

The Lady who intervenes
In the Trinity assumes
Her rights on a side altar,
A great wick that no flame lames
In a quiet arch of candle flames.

And over the dim paving
Where drowned lights are stepping stones.
In the cave of the nave,
Soled with silence that stir like water
Or whispers of prayer the women falter.

Slowly, glimmering
One after one for a moment in that still arch
Each putting a penny in the money box,
Each lights a candle and burns there
As if she'd set it to her hair.

Then one after one each woman grows
Anonymous;
They pass and are the past;
O sighing history
Shuffling by that knee!

Candles will die for their small
Concepts of virginity but she
Older than the vine sits always in the sun
Turning on all the one face
Full of grace.

Moon to what sun?
Mother of one Son
Shall I turn my back upon you and walk out?
Ere I with women find you inside me –
A tree, a growing reverie?

A great reverie
Drinking a thousand roots in me,
Growing till it opens my skull. Who then
Will gather me up
When I flower at the top?

II

Her hands are not tangible;
Her face drifts; and over all
Her body is the quality of distance
And the shine of water.

If guesses were gods,
How they would stride out towards her, seven leagues in each
        boot!
If gods are guesses, I am still moderate
In thinking they'd reach heaven through her thought.

How the heavens depend on her!
If her weather altered it would mean
Angels and their wide glories would drip from the air,
Melting in a bright shower round her like rain.

How be intimate with this
Translucent Atlas? Yet sometimes I awake
Softly as if I had been kissed
And blessed, to feel the earth quake.

Mater Dei

In March the seed
Fell, when the month leaned over, looking
Down into her valley.
And none but the woman knew it where she sat
In the tree of her veins and tended him
The red and ripening Adam of the year.

Her autumn was late and human.
Trees were nude, the lights were on the pole
All night when he came,
Her own man;
In the cry of a child she sat, not knowing
That this was a stranger.

Milk ran wild
Across the heavens. Imperiously He
Sipped at the delicate beakers she proffered him.
How was she to know
How huge a body she was, how she corrected
The very tilt of the earth on its new course?

Magna Mater

A dove plus an
Assenting virgin is
An odd equation; the bird of Venus, the
Shotsilk woodhaunter and
A country shawl
In congress to produce
The least erotic of the gods.

Afoot on Sunday, walking green
The little roads or high
In the spring carts, they come to Mass;
Hundreds who know man,
For whom no string was plucked
Or any heaven
Thrown open;

No dichotomy
Affects the prayer;
That heaven
Should have one love, and earth another seems
Entirely natural.
What Troubadour
Built this country chapel?

And out of what
Substance? Harping on what nerves?
Mothers here
All virgin, fathers none,
The child a gift of heaven
And held in common by
Each virgin mother.

O indestructible
Country mulch the Muses tread
So delicately, into the earth you go
Breeding, tending
Where flowers are born with the names of kings
You never heard of, pagan fellows
Whose histories and business
Are open secrets in your
Sunshining faces.

Coat of Arms

On Sundays the marvel
Was there early, like
A white stag in the grazing. Up the long
Lane to the belfry we children hung
On the feet of an old Mass-going man;
And it was making;
It was our turn to be looked upon

As if for once we
Had some distinction, the fields unyoked and
Turned loose, all occupation gone
But the business of man
In the holy city
That had no spires
Visible or choirs, a faint angelic land.

Nevertheless we
Stand there in a tree of neighbours,
Our feet in the
Broken artery of a bog village
Till the bell summoned us
To the other side of
The walled world that could be ours.

And I am already afraid
And suffering a mystery
That turns cold the faces the summer sun
Edges gold;
The strong are down upon their knees,
The ogham heads are
Bowed to the happenings on an altar stone.

Heraldic the
Manwoman who
Feeds the fire there, dilating into
Hands that lift, bless, flow:
We belong to a journey into air;
Bell and gong
Announce our presences elsewhere.

Come back.
I sweat at the side
Of Sunday man, feeling the static shake
In a tide of invocations. Now Monday seems
Most kindly for its implements
And farm animals, all men
At home in the homely house of flesh

Drudging in stone fields
Or high on the creeled cart marketing.

Miracle is
The priest's portion
And the Latin
That came down the muletracks where Hannibal
Stalled with his elephants.

It ends;
Missa est, and
What was to be accomplished is done;
Deflates with the harmonium;
But not quite, for out there
Hanging in the blue or
Alighted in the unyoked fields is a Sunday air

Mild and
Antlered in trees, that follows
And retreats, that will neighbour us
All day, our playfellow
And almost come to hand;
And begone by tomorrow when
Monday takes over the land.

The Skellig Way

The March crow furnishes his twig
In the knowledge that a bigger bird
Above the blow
Is hatching out the whole raw yolk of spring.

There's no Lent in the twitching rookery;
Pair by pair they go,
Feather to feather married;
Easter the nodal point in the earth's revolution.

Listen, you dumb stone faces to the West,
You on Skellig Michael,
White hoods of God,
Hermits abounding in the unseen graces,

Matins, and Lauds and Vespers are sung here
In a loud vernacular
Above the trees;
Can you do better down on your knees?

LOUIS MacNEICE (1907-1963)

The Preacher

He carried a ball of darkness with him, unrolled it
To find his way by in streets and rooms,
Every train or boat he took was Charon's ferry,
He never left the Catacombs;

He never smiled but spun his strands of black
Among the secular crowd who, when he tripped their feet
Saw their own faces in the wet street, saw
Their hell beneath the street.

Among old iron, cinders, sizzling dumps,
A world castrated, amputated, trepanned,
He walked in the lost acres crying 'Repent
For the Kingdom of Death is at hand.'

He took the books of pagan art and read
Between the lines or worked them out to prove
Humanism a palimpsest and God's
Anger a more primal fact than love.

And in the city at night where drunken song
Climbed the air like tendrils of vine
He bared a knife and slashed the roots and laid
Another curse on Cain. The sign

Of the cross between his eyes, his mouth drawn down,
He passed the flower-sellers and all
The roses reeked of an abattoir, the gardenias
Became the decor of a funeral.

His hands were always clenched, an eagle
Riveted on a world of vice;
Going upstairs he built, block upon block,
An Aztec pyramid of sacrifice.

Going upstairs to die in a bare room
He tried to square his accounts; lying in bed
He summoned home his deeds, drew back
Sixty years' expanded thread,

Pulled it in through the chink beneath the door,
Wrapped it around him, all
His faith and his despair a ball of black
And he himself at the centre of the ball

Prayer in Mid-Passage

O Thou my monster, Thou my guide,
Be with me where the bluffs divide
Nor let me contemplate return
To where my backward chattels burn
In haunts of friendship and untruth –
The Cities of the Plain of Youth.

O pattern of inhuman good,
Hard critic of our thought and blood,
By whose decree there is no zone
Where man can live by men alone,
Unveil Thyself that all may see
Thy fierce impersonality.

We were the past – and doomed because
We were a past that never was;
Yet grant to men that they may climb
This time-bound ladder out of time
And by our human organs we
Shall thus transcend humanity.

Take therefore, though Thou disregard
This prayer, this hymn, this feckless word,
O Thou my silence, Thou my song,
To whom all focal doubts belong
And but for whom this breath were breath –
Thou my meaning, Thou my death.

———————

JOHN HEWITT (1907-1987)

The Heart of Joy

The silence of the world's despair
hung round proud Caesar's empty day,
and though with drum and trumpet blare
he sought to drive the fear away,
the silence flooded back again
into the lonely hearts of men.

The legions marched; the circus roared,
but with a shudder at the heart;
the feasters thumped upon the board,
but that despair would not depart;
the silence of the world's despair
lay like an ocean everywhere.

And most men moved as puppets move,
though here and there, one seemed to wait
some sign or spectacle to prove
a core of justice in his fate;
yet not by science or by art
could any ease the stricken heart.

But on a winter midnight, far
from Caesar's tossed and troubled bed,
a shining choir, a sudden star,
a messenger light-garmented,
called down to Kings and simple men
to bid them fill their hearts again;

for, in a village stable near
the Child was born whose Grace should bring
an end to man's despair and fear,
a Maiden's Son and Heaven's King;
for God himself had taken on
man's tribulations in His Son.

And so that point where time began,
flows back and forward from was there,
where mortal as the bravest man,
God faced the ultimate despair;

no other means could he employ
to prove the heart of life is joy.

Carol Singers
for Deirdre

Why should it stir me, when, each face intent,
the Christmas children sing my childhood back,
clustered with hollied memories, innocent,
that lie discarded on my lonely track?

The walk in frost and darkness to the church,
doubling my steps to match my father's stride,
the greetings and the handshakes in the porch –
to be held that faith, I think until he died.

That faith, that story, half the stuff of art,
the myth, the magic of the Holy Child –
why should such sadness gather round my heart,
when every sense reports it unfulfilled,
its terms decayed, its uses out of date
as easel-painting or my classroom slate?

Evangelist

And now and then a loud evangelist
might come to plead, to threaten and alarm,
but though he'd thump the pulpit with his fist
the big thick Bible came to little harm.
It was in corrugated mission halls
the masters of this craft gained most success.
In our grandparents' days such strident calls
drew hundreds to surrender and confess,
rise penitent, redeemed, to step transformed
from pews where we now shifted, ill at ease;
no citadel of Satan here was stormed;
only that deaf old man in the front pew
habitually groaned upon his knees,
the last to Wesley's inspiration true.

———————

DENIS DEVLIN (1908-1959)

The Passion of Christ
to Allen Tate

The Fall

From what did man fall?
From the Archangel Michael's irritated wing?
Man is so small,
Without him first the universe did sing,
So fortunate since the Christ endued his caul:
Let us take on the whole
Story in its negligence and passion –
Archangel, we your images that fall,
Dissolve and reassemble, session by session,
You rise and rise, God's wasp, and sting!
We fall and rise, God's instrument, and sing!

The Garden of Eden

Leaving the Garden, our first father stayed
Behind, and wept, and death is still delayed.

The Man of Sorrows

He sought our sorrow out and brought it back
From merchants in the back streets of the heart:
But we, suspended between love and lack,
    Will neither sign off nor take part.

The Annunciation

What we have best imagined is the Mother
Who, with the absolute, say Light, brought forth
Self, without intervention of the Other,
    The pure, the Virgin birth.

Gabriel, death-borne on shaking, human knees,
Humorously settles down,
Deriding with his infinite, mad eyes
    Our market risk, our saints' unknown.

The Nativity

We are told how the Son of Man was born,
    Known to His Father, Who never
Recognises birth or death; and how the worn
    World's to be His breath forever.

Christ Takes Leave of His Mother

He, Who was born of Her that knew not Nature,
Yet with shut fists weeps like Nature's creature;
The black skies resent their shuddering wings,
And what was heavenly weeps, what natural sings.

Christ's Entry into Jerusalem

Open the gates and welcome in the Lord!
His sweet brow and invisible sword.

Now the palms wither, and the arch
Befriends no more the trulls' and porters' march.

Caesar takes the show seriously –
But Christ is serious with a world to free.

Christ Expels the Merchants from the Temple

The salesmen of ideas fake their list,
Worse than the trulls and their traffickers!
Again and again He strikes them off the list –
Again and again they claim the place as theirs.

Washing of the Feet

With false and annual humility,
Contracting singular love into its type,
The Pharisees extend their feet, which He
In saintly rage will wash, and even wipe!

The Last Supper

None of us can remember without tears
Nor asking with what faculty we failed:
Was it the purse, or Peter's doubting ears?
    Or the rash brethren jailed?

And when Judas wiped his mouth with bread:
What horror was it raised our loyal arm?
The small room was filled with all the dead;
And Christ broke bread and broke the mortal charm.

Outside the window, the world was still,
Absence of principalities and powers:
    The world His will,
He broke and said He would be ours.

The Agony in the Garden

Peter and James and John.
Though the fox find shelter and the swollen famished dog
And in His dispensation sleep the innocent log,
Yet the Lord finds no breast to lean upon.

Peter and James and John.
Olive branches mime against the moonlight
All natural agitation from sound to sight:
Yet there is not pain enough in Nature for Him to reason on.

Peter and James and John.
It is not angels He wants, nor fallen angels even, but men
To wear down, if only in Time, that unnatural pain;
Not active Peter, nor neutral James, nor passive John.

Christ before the Magistrates

By now the Church and State have had their fling,
The generous flesh is pared to the bone:
Christ and Caesar come to the same thing,
    The scorned and scornful soul, their own.

There will be something more when this is over,
The Lion and the Lamb adopt His voice,
    Beloved submit to lover,
Kneel down, and then stand up and rejoice!

Veronica's Veil

They tend His fierce divinity, shy saviours,
From the calvaries of the dispossessed,
Ragged mothers who give milk to their neighbours
While the husband fails, and the child undressed

Scrabbles at the empty plate, some holy women
Will take their last white linen from the drawer
And saying: 'God is ours as He is human,'
Wipe the blood from the unbearable scar.

Before Pilate

To flagellate, to crown with thorns, to make
A show of man who would Man create –
Nothing much when Justice is at stake –
The conflict of laws idly becomes Fate.

The scene's complete! the filthy, wine-lit bands,
Forgive Barabbas who shed blood,
Pilate, the surgeon, cleans his distant hands,
In sage disgust, praises the Good.

Way of the Cross

At every stage along that station,
Averted eyes, reluctant heart!
Mob hatred, Pharisees' elation –
His knees watery from the start,

One, Simon, in excess of passion,
Trusted his unreflecting hands;
What is this genius of compassion
That comprehends, nor understands!

At Calvary

Axes shone in the sunlight
Where sound and sight from one source came;
Christ was striking at the roots
Whence grew our birthright and its name,

The reason that was perfect gave
The round, simple, pagan sun:
What was humanity to save
The tears of Christ in the machine?

Lifted on the Cross

There's little certain – but no doubt
Eternity in Time's put out!

There may be lights over the plain,
That's where some acolytes, mad and sane,

Mad for life and sane for death;
Centurion! crown these ribs of wrath!

The Cross

Two thieves – why two? to make three criminals?
How dare the centre judge the left and right
Judging: 'You shall be with Me in Paradise'
Judging: 'You shall be in Hell for life'
If I were one of those two casual thieves
And spied on our degraded bloody Lord:
How could I know how to pronounce the Word,
The Word that doubts, the Word that believes?

The Good Thief

It is not right for me to talk to You,
To wait on You with ministerial bow,
To pray, or if I lived in higher merit
To love even, or to adore, or care.
Why? the reasons? there are many of them;
    That You are there and are not there.

The huge and foreign universes round me,
The small dishonours in me coat my heart:
Whether the whim of the ignoble beast
Or the Gothic nobility of the choir,
It makes no difference, both high and low,
    Are burned to nothing in Your fire.

My will You will for a fire towards You
Dies without my kindling, or is quenched
In unguided storms from Your high quarters:
My memory in lethargy turns sour
All whence, my understanding less imperious
    Day by day and hour by hour,

Loses whole continents where in my childhood
I was Your Viceroy, and approved the Just
And condemned my natural evil thoughts –
Now, what has changed me? Is it the years

You made and gave me, Lord? or am I prone to the evil
   The masters dinned into my ears?

Praise and recrimination sit well on us
Whose quality's defined by life and death;
But nothing, neither life or death adorns us
Like adoration of our Lord, the Christ,
No buildings, no culture of roses, no bridges
   Like the majesty of Christ.

The Bad Thief

Lord, we You've made it in our power
To destroy the World You saved us in
And not only our bodies with Your souls,
Your soul created for Your praise forever
But all that has been made against Your image
   Passes, both now and never,

Beasts that eat their young in innocence,
Men that torture knowing what they do –
Innocent things and conscientious things –
We who destroy the flower and the grass,
The thrush whose song's as powerful as the sea
   All this and more has come to pass.

Ascension

It happens through the blond window, the trees
With diverse leaves divide the light, light birds;
Aengus, the God of Love, my shoulders brushed
With birds, you could say lark or thrush or thieves

And not be right yet – or ever right –
For it was God's Son foreign to our moor:
When I looked out the window, all was white,
And what's beloved in the heart was sure,

With such a certainty ascended He,
The Son of Man who deigned Himself to be:
Then when we lifted out of sleep, there was
Life with its dark, and love above the laws.

96

Transfiguration

All is as if that Face transpired with Light
As if dark were light
As if wrong were right
The torsion and the tension of that Night!

The world opens like a door: Come in!
Body is in the way,
Soul is waste and play,
Oh, come, Unworldly, from the World within!

Lough Derg

The poor in spirit on their rosary rounds,
The jobbers with their whiskey-angered eyes,
The pink bank clerks, the tip-hat papal counts,
And drab, kind women their tonsured mockery tries,
Glad invalids on penitential feet
Walk the Lord's majesty like their village street.

With mullioned Europe shattered, this Northwest,
Rude-sainted isle would pray it whole again:
(Peasant Apollo! Troy is worn to rest.)
Europe that humanised the sacred bane
Of God's chance who yet laughed in his mind
And balanced thief and saint: were they this kind?

Low rocks, a few weasels, lake
Like a field of burnt gorse; the rooks caw,
Ours, passive, for man's gradual wisdom take
Firefly instinct dreamed out into law;
The prophets' jewelled kingdom down at heel
Fires no Augustine here. Inert, they kneel;

All is simple and symbol in their world,
The incomprehended rendered fabulous.
Sin teases life whose natural fruits withheld
Sour the deprived nor bloom for timely loss:
Clan Jansen! less what magnanimity leavens
Man's wept-out, fitful, magniloquent heavens

97

Where prayer was praise, O Lord! the Temple trumpets
Cascaded down Thy sunny pavilions of air
The scroll-tongued priests, the galvanic strumpets,
All clash and stridency gloomed upon Thy stair;
The pharisees, the exalted boy their power
Sensually psalmed in Thee, their coming hour!

And to the sun, earth turned her flower of sex,
Acanthus in the architects' limpid angles;
Close priests allegorised the Orphic egg's
Brood, and from the Academy, tolerant wranglers
Could hear the contemplatives of the Tragic Choir
Drain off man's sanguine, pastoral death-desire.

It was said stone dreams and animal sleeps and man
Is awake; but sleep with its drama on us bred
Animal articulate, only somnambulist can
Conscience like Cawdor give the blood its head
For the dim moors to reign through druids again.
O first geometer! tangent-feelered brain

Clearing by inches the encircled eyes
Bolder than the peasant tiger whose autumn beauty
Sags in the expletive kill, or the sacrifice
Of dearth puffed positive in the stance of duty
With which these pilgrims would propitiate
Their fears; no leafy, medieval state

Of paschal cathedrals backed on earthy hooves
Against the craftsmen's primary-coloured skies
Whose gold was Gabriel on the patient roofs,
The parabled windows taught the dead to rise,
And Christ the Centaur, in two natures whole,
With fable and proverb joinered body and soul.

Water withers from the oars. The pilgrims blacken
Out of the boats to masticate their sin
Where Dante smelled among the stones and bracken
The door to Hell (O harder Hell where pain
Is earthed, a casuist sanctuary of guilt!).
Spirit bureacracy on a bet built

Part by this race when monks in convents of coracles
For the Merovingian centuries left their land,
Belled, fragrant; and honest in their oracles
Bespoke the grace to give without demand,
Martyrs Heaven winged nor tempted with reward.
And not ours, doughed in dogma, who never have dared

Will with surrogate palm distribute hope:
No better nor worse than I who, in my books,
Have angered at the stake with Bruno and by the rope
Watt Tyler swung from, leagued with shifty looks
To fuse the next rebellion with the desperate
Serfs in the sane need to eat and get;

Have praised, on its thunderous canvas, the Florentine smile
As man took to wearing his death, his own
Sapped crisis through cathedral branches (while
Flesh groped loud round dissenting skeleton)
In soul, reborn as body's appetite:
Now languish back in body's amber light,

Now is consumed. O earthly paradise!
Hell is to know our natural empire used
Wrong, by mind's moulting, brute divinities.
The vanishing tiger's saved, his blood transfused.
Kent is for Jutes again and Glasgow town
Burns high enough to screen the stars and moon.

Well may they cry who have been robbed, their wasting
Shares in justice legally lowered until
Man his own actor, matrix, mold and casting,
Or man, God's image, sees his idol spill.
Say it was pride that did it, or virtue's brief:
To them that suffer it is no relief.

All indiscriminate, man, stone, animal
Are woken up in nightmare. What John the Blind
From Patmos saw works and we speak it. Not all
The men of God nor the priests of mankind
Can mend or explain the good and broke, not one
Generous with love prove communion.

Behind the eyes the winged ascension flags,
For want of spirit by the market blurbed,
And if hands touch, such fraternity sags
Frightened this side the dykes of death disturbed
Like Aran Islands' bibulous, unclean seas:
Pietà: but the limbs ache; it is not peace.

Then to see less, look little, let hearts' hunger
Feed on water and berries. The pilgrims sing:
Life will fare well from elder to younger,
Though courage fail in a world-end, rosary ring.
Courage kills its practitioners and we live,
Nothing forgotten, nothing to forgive.

We pray to ourself. The metal moon, unspent
Virgin eternity sleeping in the mind,
Excites the form of prayer without content;
Whitethorn lightens, delicate and blind,
The negro mountain, and so, knelt on her sod,
This woman beside me murmuring *My God! My God!*

FRANCIS MacMANUS (1909-1965)

Ascent of the Reek

Pilgrims, O pilgrims, where are you going?
Up to the Reek, to the holy man's mountain.
Keep your stick in your fist or you'll tumble forever,
tumble and toss with the torrents of water,
water that's brown with the bog's bitter drainings,
water that scours out the rocks like a penance.
But Patrick keeps guard from the cold windy summit,
watching with prayer like the sunrise about him,
his *casula* wet with the labour of sorrow,
his bell hoarse with ringing damnation to demons,
for fear we should fail, we the nation he fashioned;
watching forever, his eyes never weary,
wrestling with devils and angels and Heaven,
he, who accounted himself sinner of sinners.

Pilgrims, O pilgrims, how far to the summit?
Now our breath breaks like the shudder of death,
now the sharp stones are an ambush of demons,
now the cold morning cuts heat from our hearts.

Pilgrims, O pilgrims, the darkness is lifting,
daybreak is polishing ocean's dulled mirror,
islands will gleam like the rivets on silver.
But prayers must be said till the heart groans in anguish,
limbs must be strained till the flesh is no rebel,
bones must be tried till the will is the master,
slopes must be climbed till the body is civil.
Thirst is a prayer that makes the tongue kindle;
hunger a penance that cries in the belly.
Pilgrims, O pilgrims, look down on the ocean,
morning uncovers the islands to glory.

Pilgrims, O pilgrims, here is your haven.
Lost are the torrents spuming sour water;
below is the bog that hugged the heels evilly;
below are the boulders that huddled to hinder us;
below are the flints that dared us and prattled.
But look at that man who bares his knees bravely,
kneels to the stones while his mouth utters Aves.
(God save ye, pilgrims, here Patrick guards us)

Look at that woman, old as the mountain,
swinging her beads to the shake of her fingers.
(Patrick is watching over all Ireland)
Look at that girl who skips like a sparrow,
brown as a berry, laughing and gabbing.
Patrick he guards them all from his mountain,
guarding with prayers like these strong winds about him,
his *casula* wet with the love that melts heaven,
his bell beating devils to rout in infernos,
for fear we should fail, we his nation, his people,
watching for ever, his eyes like the planets,
Patrick the slave and the master of Ireland.

Pilgrims, O pilgrims, whence are you coming?
Back from Croagh Patrick's mountain high vigil.
Back from the flight of the darkness at morning.
Back from a word to the maker of Ireland.

Lent

Mary Magdalene, that easy woman,
Saw, from the shore, the seas
Beat against the hard stone of Lent,
Crying, 'Weep, seas, weep
For yourselves that cannot dent me more.

O more than all these, more crabbed than all stones,
And cold, make me, who once
Could leap like water, Lord. Take me
As one who owes
Nothing to what she was. Ah, naked

My waves of scent, my petticoats of foam
Put from me and rebut;
Disown. And that salt lust stave off
That slavered me – O
Let it whiten in grief against the stones

And outer reefs of me. Utterly doff,
Nor leave the lightest veil
Of feeling to heave or soften.
Nothing cares this heart
What hardness crates it now or coffins.

Over the balconies of these curved breasts
I'll no more peep to see
The light procession of my loves
Surf-riding in to me
Who now have eyes and alcove, Lord, for Thee.'

'Room, Mary,' said He, 'ah make room for me
Who am come so cold now
To my tomb.' So, on Good Friday
Under a frosty moon
They carried Him and laid Him in her womb.

A grave and icy mask her heart wore twice,
But on the third day it thawed,

And only a stone's-flow away
Mary saw her God.
Did you hear me? Mary saw her God!

Dance, Mary Magdalene, dance, dance and sing,
For unto you is born
This day a King. 'Lady,' said He,
'To you who relent
I bring back the petticoat and the bottle of scent.'

The Trinity

Down the darkened hall of brain
Darts the tiny mouse of pain,
Quick as thought the waking cat
Of consciousness scoots from the mat,

Elastically catches it,
Statically lets it go
Slack again, but snatches it
Lightly back in its yo-yo.

Till in the vast and breathing hall
A thousand sleepers wake and call
'Curse the cat and curse the mouse,
– And curse, God curse, this bloody house.'

God who did send this I to cry
Between two selves on Calvary,
God who in darkness all forlorn
Between two thieving moods was torn,

(The nagging cat of thought, the mouse
Of niggling guilt that runs this house)
Make these two malefactors one
Within this I
That soon must die,
And then will rise the Sun, the Sun,
The trinity, the three-in-one.

Nativity

His holly hair, his berry eyes are here,
And his chrysanthemum wound,
This Christmas day; by symbols once again
The Mystery's importuned.

Hisses the singing kettle of his blood
Out of his sanguine side,
Poked by the sibling spear it ebbs and flows
In a hub-bubble tide

That dyes the silent room. The gay young god,
Dog in the manger now,
Growls in the hearth, and bares old teeth against
The Ass in us, the Cow.

There are the portly bottle-loins, and there
The wine-marks of his birth
Upon the straw, the biscuit-brittle straw
Broken by Mary's girth.

And here, most meek, most eager and most hushed,
The angelic agents hover,
A great prudential company, all come
To offer him life-cover.

Comes sentiment with frozen tears lent
By memory, melting sweet,
Her hothead cries boil over and congeal
Again at her cold feet.

And Grief, deep in her crushed and tinfoil wrap,
Brokenly glares today
Among the ashes and the cruel butt-
Ends of this Christmas play.

And there's the tapering tree of his descent,
Hitched to a kingly star,
Earth is its horizontal, heaven and hell
Its upright centre-spar.

The very tree of life, so base, so wide,
And with such longing fraught,
Up the step-ladder of our looks it spires
Into a point of thought.

In the stark winter of our tinselled pride
Its frozen growth now stands
Waiting the fiery gift, the melting dew
Spangled from heavenly hands.

Ah look! the bush is candelabraed now
With yellow and with blue,
Types of the spirit, sweet and bitter both,
Opposed but wholly true.

Outside, like rootless souls the silent trees
Sail past on trays of mist;
The miser-circle on the pane still marks
The place that Judas kissed.

His thistle breath still lingers in the air,
Spiky with eagerness,
It hovers on the garden, and the grass
Whitens at his caress.

Robin with rusty bib no longer can
Pull out the worm-like nail,
Dumpy with impotence it droops and humps
Upon the wooden rail.

And hark! the Herod-angels sing tonight!
Over the Magi's tents
Their heartless song drones on through grumbling glooms
And weeping continents.

High on his farthing floor the airman moons
Above the mourning town
Of Bethlehem; it is his fiddling root
And he the flower and crown.

O Caspar, Melchior, and Balthazar,
Come from your caravan
And tell me where you go, and what new star
You saw in Teheran:

And what new man now hurries to be born
Out of our addled earth,
And O what silly corner of ourselves
Will see the mangy birth.

Strike, strike the gong of our song till souls take fire,
Clap hands and bellow,
Dance, dance, leap higher and longer, and hug
Each with its fellow.

Lord, in this wintry interval we send
Our indolent regards
And grey regrets. Make fluent all the pens
Of all the frozen bards.

Lay the live coal upon their lips that they
May leap uproariously
Out of their huff of words, and let the thorns
Crackle with prophecy.

Resume, and reimburse the silent wood,
Elaborate its saps,
Bid the bare trees blurt into bloom, and fill
With leaf the hungry gaps,
And in its head set the heart's singing birds.

Resurrection

An Easter Sequence

'O vos omnes,
Qui transitis per viam, attendite, et videte,
Si est dolor similis sicut dolor meus,
Attendite universi populi, et videte
                    dolorem meum, dolorem meum.'

Tell ye the daughter of Sion. Behold thy King cometh unto thee...

It was a deliberate moment, and O
Just in the nick and nook of time he came,
The timeless One, to reclaim us. Everything waited,

106

Everything peaked and pointed to his coming.
The morning rose up early, a tip toe of a day,
All was light and elastic, the birds chirping away,
The air chipped into buds. People were on their kness
With wonder, and some were weeping. And when at last He appeared
– The Hero – such a hail of huzzas and hosannahs as sprang up!
Why, the very house-tops rose to the occasion and broke
Their hush and hung out all their hearts' hoorays.
This was glory. Yet, he knew the swings of men, and now
It was the old story.
The day too bright to last, the crowd too loud to stay.
Those who magnified now would mock Him tomorrow,
Those who defied, defy. Already He saw
The shadow of Doubt, the pickpocket of conviction,
Move through the crowd. And far away and behind
Their fume and furore of glory he heard the door
Of doom slam; meanwhile all was gay
And like a King he came triumphant up this way.

And when He was come into Jerusalem, all the city
  was moved, saying Who is this?

It was no day at all for doubt or for cloud,
The children ran cheering in front, the birds sang loud,
The very trees were bowed; and the butterfly leaves
Took off to greet him.
But he rode loftily by as if uninvolved in the glory,
And the ass, as if understanding the story,
Carried him sadly on to a tame
And lamentable conclusion.
To meet with all and go with none
That was his doom who mediates and makes one
The split that was in man since time began.

But how to heal the breach? how to reach across?
Ay, that was the only answer now – the Cross!
Deep in his mind the roots ran that way, and his fate
Was fixed. The tree was grown that stood on Calvary,
What was to do was done. Still, it was a glad day,
Let the bells all ring, let them have their fling,
For this way led to glory and to everlasting Spring.

Now when the even was come, he sat down with the twelve.

> Twelve heads hugged in a ring
> Twelve hands breaking bread
> Twelve hearts bursting to sing
> The song of life from the dead.

Now the moment had come; he must love them and leave them
Yet without losing; this is the mystery of losing.
In the world, of course, it is different; there, every love of life
Of person, place, or thing, is a boon and a beauty
That comes in the morning so freely. Yet, in the afternoon,
Fearful of losing it we freeze it into a duty
And judge it our due. And then what surprise
When in the evening it dies.
O if only we had faith enough not to confine
And coffin the thing that we love, faith enough to receive
It just when it came, insight enough to let go and believe
That each morning would bring it again,
We would not have to grieve over the thing that was slain.
So he spoke to them at supper, so he figured it forth
In the breaking of bread
To those who were his twelve selves, dear as his own soul.
For all these selves his soul had for sieves
To let fall his story
As snow falls in flakes; yet who knows if it gives
One half of what it knows of the whole glory.

And as they did eat, he said, Verily I say unto you, that
  one of you shall betray me.

Name him not, Name him not, nor constellate
The one who led him to his fate. Nevertheless
Judas was part of Jesus.
For the god has always a foot of clay, and the soul
Grows in soil, the flower has a dark root.
And deep in all is the base collaborator.
The betrayer is ever oneself, never another.
All must say, 'Lord, is it I?' There is always
Evil in Goodness, lust in love, dust on the dove's foot,
And without it purity's groundless. And the Cross
Had never been.

Then cometh Jesus with them unto a place called Gethsemane.

It was a lovely night,
A night for weddings and for water.
Going out into the cold glow he felt washed
And clean of people. The garden had an air
Of waiting about it, as if the leaves were bent
On eavesdropping. And the rain
Scented the air with more-than-midnight pain
And the wet trees that had nowhere to go
Stood round and gazed at the One walking there below
In agony. Ebb and flow, to and fro, Yes and No;
Doubt assailed him. Which and what to do? This much must be
    admitted,
We lie between two worlds, faith and doubt,
Like breath. The air that one breathes does not care
Whether it's in or out; it's not in love with life
Or death. And yet we do not dare to hold·it long,
But must let go to find again. So with faith,
With love, with everything. Now at the cross-roads,
Middled and muddled he stood.
This was it. And it was night. 'Nevertheless Thy will be done.'
That thought made morning of it, gave him ease, and issue.
He knew now how to stay and stare it out
And already the torches approached the garden.

Now Peter sat without in the Palace.

Tenebrae now; and quenched as if by doubt
One after one the torches all go out
In token of the twelve who went away
Each after other on the fatal day.
That fateful night,
Late in the palace, something strange occurred.
A spider lit on his hand, and he threw it away
But it returned to his hand on a thread;
He threw it away again, and again away;
And again till his fingers were dripping
And webbed with threads, but, horrible! still it came back
Like a truth that could not be denied;
Peter desisted. He listened. In the cold dawn
The cock was throwing aloft its threefold crown
And aureole of sound. Then he remembered
The meaning.

In the dark blue and petering hour
Of night it sang, and looking out,
He saw the tree dance into flower
Enlisting all the morning's light;
It was the bloody Judas tree,
And on it hung not him, but *me*.

Which of the twain will ye that I release unto you?
They said Barabbas.

We will always beg the question.
Jesus did not belong to this time;
Their clocks all said he came before his chime,
All the lamps of the city declared him a stranger,
A nobody come out of darkness, and therefore a danger
To law and to order. Must it always be so?
Must we always make light of the devil we know
And dark of the god who is ranger? O stranger
It is easy to choose what's dead right, right
— So we say — to refuse to live wrong; so we move
In thick circles of self, and the lean dog-rose
Looks for the hole in our hedge and lurks
In our thorn waiting to leap out of lack
Into bloom like the god in the manger.

And when he had scourged Jesus, he delivered him to be crucified.

They took him out to die.
The lark was shaking out its acres of song in the sky
And the sun shone. People looked up and remarked
What a wonderful day it was going to be
And the cheering boys ran on in front of the crowd,
And the cheeky ones waited to stare.
Once he noticed

A blind man whom he had healed looking at him
With horrified eyes as much as to say
'Was it for this I was given sight by the god that day?'
He turned away. If only this had been an important death,
If only he knew that the people who barracked him now
Had been travelling years and years to reach this place.
But they were casual passers-by and their interest was jaded.
Yet it was all as he had expected, and
He would not avoid or evade it. Far away

110

A spool of birds was spinning above the hill,
And still Pilate sat in the empty court beneath,
Sucking threads of thoughtfulness through his teeth.

And they crucified him.

This was a rough death, there was nothing tidy about it,
No sweetness, nothing noble.
Everything stuck out awkwardly and angular:
The clumsy soldier brought the wrong basket of nails;
And the couriers — those sticky fly-papers of events —
Did not even bother to cover his sticky end,
Or carry it home to Rome. For them the war in Gaul
Was more important; the ship of state sailed on,
Leaving him bogging in the backward seas.
Still, that is how things always happen, lousily,
But later on, the heart edits them lovingly,
Abstracts the jeers and jags, imports a plan
Into the pain, and calls it history.
We always go back to gloss over some roughness,
To make the past happen properly as we want it to happen.
But this was a hard death. At the time
There was no room for thought.
How often he had hearsed and rehearsed this hour.
But when you come up against it all the good words about it
Are less than breath. It is hard to turn the other cheek
When both have been slapped:
                              Yes, it was a hard death.

Now there stood by the Cross of Jesus his mother . . .

A mist opened and closed its eyes before him,
And in it he saw her looking at him
The untouchable terrible god.
O what ladders of longing led up from her
To him, what steps and depths of memory ran down;
He remembered the happy days in Galilee
When he was heaven's hub; the heap of smoking grass,
The bubble-pipe, the light upon the wall,
The children in the far garden looking for the lost ball,
And Mary calling him. He was always so distant
In those lonely days. O if only
He had mattered less, she wondered, if only
She had mastered him more, would he then

Have been like other men, a flat satisfied plain?
But no. In him mountains of onlyness rose
Snow-high. Dayspring was in his eyes
At midnight. And he would not come down
From his far purpose even for her who was
The root that raised him to this Cross and crown
Of thorns. Yet tenderly he spoke
Goodbye now, his voice choking and dry.
And as she went away, leaving him to die,
The vast moon of his cry rose up upon the darkness.
His heart broke.

*About the ninth hour Jesus cried with a loud voice, saying, Eli, Eli,
lama sabacthani?*

His breath came in threads; his words were not his own.
He was dying now.
The sun refused to look, and the sky
Closed up its eye. Only the windows of his wounds
Were wide open, and the red curtains of blood
Blew out into the storm, torn to ribbons.
He could no longer fend death off.
Slow, slow, loath to go, hope holds up its head
Though feet are so sawn through, like a sawn tree that stands
Long, then with one blinding run and blundering tear
Of last despair, scattering its brains and branches on the air
Slumps, lumps, pitches headlong and thuds, a log clodded clean.
So his last cry and acquiescence. And the vast wall
Of people drew back before that dying fall.
God was dead.

*And, behold, the veil of the temple was rent in twain from the top to
the bottom; and the earth did quake and the rocks rent;*

Now was the world's back broken; the darkness
Heaved in half, the wells rose up in walls
And fell in floods; and earth's own gorge
Rose and retched out its coffins. Everywhere
Lightnings lashed, and the curled thunder rolled
Its bolts over the crowd that broke and ran before its crash.
Each flash showed them in a different flight.
And in the downpour only the soldiers stood
Sodden and awed beneath the Cross. 'This was the son of God!'

To them the eliminating moment was
The illuminating one. Now all was still.
And on the desolate plain behind the hill
An ass brayed. Its palmy days were over.

*And there was Mary Magdalene and the other Mary, sitting over
against the sepulchre . . .*

It is always the women who are the Watchers
And keepers of life: they guard our exits
And our entrances. They are both tomb and womb,
End and beginning. Bitterly they bring forth
And bitterly take back the light they gave.
The last to leave and still the first to come,
They circle us like sleep or like the grave.
Earth is their element, and in it lies
The seed and silence of the lighted skies,
The seasons with their fall and slow uprise,
Man with his sight and militant surmise.
It is always the women who are the Watchers
And Wakeners.

*In the end of the Sabbath, as it began to dawn towards the first day of
the week, came Mary Magdalene.*

The tomb, the tomb, that
Was her core and care, her one sore.
The light had hardly scarleted the dark
Or the first bird sung when Mary came in sight
With eager feet. Grief, like last night's frost,
Whitened her face and tightened all her tears.
It was there, then, there at the blinding turn
Of the bare future that she met her past.
She only heard this Angel tell her how
The holding stone broke open and gave birth
To her dear Lord, and how his shadow ran
To meet him like a dog.
And as the sun
Burns through the simmering muslins of the mist
Slowly his darkened voice, that seemed like doubt,
Morninged into noon; the summering bees
Mounted and boiled over in the bell-flowers.
'Come out of your mail, Mary', he said, 'the doors are open
And joy has its ear cocked for your coming.

Earth now is no place to mope in. So throw away
Your doubt, cast every clout of care,
Hang all your hallelujahs out
This airy day.'

ROBERT FARREN (1909-1985)

Stable Straw

Straw, and figures of moulded clay,
the white-knitted hands of the men that pray
when Christian men make a holiday
for a Child, a Man, and a Lady.

The pith of our life, the ground of our awe,
the meat and the marrow of all our law,
symbolled in clay and in stable-straw:
a Child, a Man, and a Lady.

For, all the beauty of tree and wind,
and the deepest thought of the stillest mind,
are driven dust, if the soul is blind
to a Child, a Man, and a Lady.

Clerk, deck altar, and kindle light,
and beat the bell in the tower's height:
priests are vesting in clothes of white
for God who was born a baby.

Lineage

Had *I* had an inn at Bethlehem
I should have shut my door on them

Had *I* hanged for theft on Calvary
I'd been deft with mockery.

Even if I'd been on Olivet
I'd have hidden it.

I *am* the boor of Bethlehem,
the hoist Calvary clown,
I was aloft on Olivet
and cringe in the town.

Witness

I

God thou hast set thee to save me!
Upon me thine eyes!
There are eyes at my back
I cannot see, with mine eyes.

God thou art ever at watch;
I have felt thee there
when in the tempting
I saw the toad.

God thou has set thee to save me,
Why else do I flinch
slipping to sleep or wakeful
with radiant people?

Why in roomy day,
in the tight dark,
does a world withdraw
and a world show?

Why, having gorged on beaaty —
of tree, of mind, of child,
of snow, of moon, of hair,
of flesh, of singing, —
why, then, thinking of Thabor,
and from Olivet God going home,
hear I 'Manna in the desert . . .
your fathers dead'?

II

God I have found a necessity binds thee:
thou has made all things and me to be like thee;
I, with all men but thy saints, hide thy likeness,
I and all men on thine image pile mountains.

Thou, of necessity — self-known, self-loving —
seekest thine own hidden-over image;
I, in the union of faculties knowing
union with things, feel the mountains cloven
peak down to root as thy pickthrust probes them.

Thou hast put Powers between my soul and its idols.
I must break doors through walls of wings to avoid thee,
Mary's to dare at first before I can dare thee,
Jesus to urge away with all of his mercy.

Mercy, my God, where has not thy mercy met me?

III
Mercy has flowed from the eyes of thy saints,
from thy Bride's praising;
from shame; from falling-away of friends;
their staying;
from brawling poster, from ghoulish print and picture
nosed out in morgue and brothel and thieves' kitchen;
from shuddering death snapped up for a scoop over rivals,
printing-presses a-roar in the judgment silence.

IV
Mercy has flowed in a thought of dread
for men never met,
never known:
men
blasted by fire; bombed; smashed in mines;
lost in the crumpling of towns;
spat from skies;
killing your own mad brains; pulped in storms;
struck in the swell of laughter —
men never met,
never known.
Gone to the silence
was any unready,
men never met,
never known?

V

Going to the silence,
unready or ready,

I can but testify
unto great mercy.
For from hourly tales of death
build I awareness,
out of love of friends turned ghosts
desire, of the eternal.
Brothers to whom I adhered,
leaving their places,
have with the gust of their flight
neared me to the angels.

VI

Glory on glory to God
for unmeasured mercy!
Justice delights in measure,
in level scales;
justice, the heart of order,
the hasp of the world.
But mercy's the child of delight,
the world's father.
Mercy makes cups flow full
and more deep to hold.

The Monks Work and Pray

And whether they prayed with the body
or prayed in the cave of the spirit,
Colm heard the whole of their praying,
(as he heard the sounds of summer
weaving and criss-crossing in the daylight
and making one sound, the summer's,)
so he heard the praying of the brethren,
as they laboured at their tasks in Iona:

Tailor asking blessing on his scissors,
weaver asking blessing on his spindle;
cobbler on his last and on his bradawl,
wheelwright on his spokes and on his flanges;
creelman on his withes and on his wattles,
herd upon his lambs, upon his cattle.
And this man figured grace as querns of granite,

117

and that one was the bellows in his smithy;
one compared his soul to corn unwinnowed,
one to a currach nosing among the Torrens;
a wheelwright pondered: 'Prayers are like true-set wheel-spokes
that keep the soul, the flange, right-round for its journey';
a beekeeper pictured Heaven a hive full of honey;
a mason cried: 'God is like stone — strong, sure, upholding.'

And Colm heard all this praying
as the shadow of the glorified body,
as a changing of body to spirit,
as a change of one world to another,
as a penetration with Godhead,
as perpetual levitation,
as conversation in Heaven.

His soul leaped in its members
like a spear driven with power,
like a spring shot from a hillside,
like fire gushed from a mountain.
He crooked on his knees to hold it,
flattened his body on the sand-dunes,
murmuring God's name like a lover,
and was wrapped in Christ's arms, in the Bridegroom's.

And O what were the fasting, and the vigils,
and the starving of desire, and the labour,
and the wading into streams like thornwoods,
and the live-long travelling through psalmbooks —
compared with the kisses of the Bridegroom,
compared with the breath of the Anointed!

As sand-dust given for amber.
As weed-ash given for gold dust.
As grass exchanged for fine raiment.

Sleep

While now I lay me down to sleep
I pray to God my soul to keep,
that, riding out with sleep to-night,
it may turn back with morning's light.

Or, if in sleep it slip my clay,
may it blaze back to that High Day
it left behind to make me man
out of the thing that flesh began . . .

Though flesh and flesh together go
and man beget and woman grow,
yet is there nothing human made
till the new spirit start its trade.

Aye, flesh can sow in flesh, and can
raise crop, but not the crop of man:
until the down-sent soul is come
no human hand or head's begun;
until the ripeness feel the soul
entice it to contrive man-bone
the passion-sown, womb-stemming plant,
bid to turn human, cannot start;
and God makes freshly each new soul,
God, the all-making God, alone.

Than, ghostly-begun by Holy Ghost,
soul to its groping man-thing gropes
and soul and thing make man. Man, born,
walks the wild, haunted world in storm,
in head's and heart's and hand's bright force;
till head, heart, hand each failing goes
earth under haunted earth to turn
down being's steps to stem and worm.
But back the perpetual soul, impelled,
hurtles to Christ, the Lustrous Head.

There then's the map, the world's design
which all forms fit – man, sleep and time.

By hand's and heart's and head's bright force
the living man through earth's life goes;
but force of hand in soul begins,
and souls have force beyond hearts' brim;
now, thought for wing, soul levitates
loose of limbs' plot of time and space;
it beats light wings through time that was,
it spans the silken seas of God,

it tips the aevum's endless start,
eternity's live, stirless heart.

Soul can conceive a thought like God's,
body its thought in verse or bronze,
rib it, add limb – of note, of stone –
just as 'God gives clay limb to soul:
old thing into unknown thing turned
soul can exalt, expand, the world.

And yet, with this high-searching soul,
man has the death-drift in the bone.
Man's spirit (breath of body's breath,
still heart of beating heart, fine weft
of fleshy weave), alive in sense,
sups on the sensuous universe.
It fans the fiery, clay-blood heart,
drifts with the senses' drift to dark,
cold to that Lustrous Head that lights
or strikes souls dark, with Paradise.

Man, the wild bee of Time, will try
to sip the world and blind an eye
and say, there seems no call to die. . .

And so God makes the body sleep
to save the soul for modesty,
rehearsing man with nightly death
to bear the frightful stop of breath.
And so God takes my soul away
and makes my world end every day;
and I, there, with shuttered eye,
a mere breathing body lie,
all-but returned to lightless womb,
all-but inhabitant of tomb:
while God upholds me in His Hand,
and if He fasten fingers hard
O I am lost or lapped in bliss
for all endless centuries!

While now I lay me down to sleep
I pray to God my soul to keep:
never to let my body die
till Christ's Body in me lie,

till Christ's Blood behind the oil
leaving anointing hand assoil
lid, and limb, and lip, and ear,
and nostril, till the spirit's clear.
Ah then I'll lay me down to sleep
and Father, Son and Spirit keep
my soul until my body leap.

Until my body leap from clay
on all mankind's Uprising Day,
and down–sent soul and body sprung
shall rise together, rung by rung,
and I that was with worm and clod
in my own flesh shall see my God.

KEVIN FALLER (1920-1983)

Nun

When she was very young
brick by brick they built
the wall around her
now she is immured in a myth

on an island in the stream
of traffic she is not
a moment closer to this city
than that lady of Shallot

it may not matter if the end
bring her to bliss or to oblivion
and yet one longs for Launcelot's
armour to storm her eyes with sun

Edel Quinn

The fire of life burns smokily
Unless a spirit blow;
And so with you, kinswoman,
The spirit made flesh glow;

I do not know the God you know
Except by word of mouth,
Mine is a little world of fear,
Uncertainty and doubt;

But I have read the life you led
Who loved the Virgin and Her Son
And shamed by you I flamed from you
Whose living breath is done.

ROY McFADDEN (1921-   )

Contemplations of Mary

I

When he said *Mary,* she did not at once
Look up to find the voice, but sat recalling
Warm patches of her childhood, and her falling
Heartoverhead in love with every glance
Of admiration crowding through the dance,
Or in the streets bent back and almost calling.

Girls put on sex like flowers; their small breasts
Emerge like blushes, knowing, innocent;
The underflow of all their ways intent
On welling up with welcome for the guests
Who darken love's white threshold. All the rest's
Above, outside, like god and government.

So she sat on when he first spoke to her.
Hearing perhaps a new sound of command,
Like parent's tug at child's reluctant hand,
Did not at once look up and answer *Sir,*
But sat with memory her conspirator,
Downcast, and did not want to understand.

But he persisted. *Mary*. She resigned
Her meadows and her rainbows to his voice,
Inevitably now, without a choice,
Surrendering all the stairways of her mind;
Then, finally bereft, was empty, blind,
Until the word bulged up and broke. *Rejoice.*

122

II

Then she was different. Her past perfect years
Seemed like another woman's purse, all strange
In ordinary things, keys, compact, change:
And home no longer nested up those stairs,
Involved with tables, pictures, cupboards, chairs.

Everything was leaning out askew
Since it had touched, no hardly touched her, blown
A strange breath through her branches and the mown
And planted garden of her private view,
Those yesterdays no longer *I* but *you.*

Was it her knowledge of the clouded womb
That crowded out her quiet corridors:
Her certainty of child? Or, like far doors
Slamming goodbyes, was it a shout of doom,
The dying of a world in her small room:

Her mind a skirt of fear ballooning back
To girlish unencumbered days when life
Required no definitions; sweetheart, wife
Made love, embroidered, lived without some lack
Of meaning like a rat at every crack:

Mary, still girl enough to twirl her hood
From birth and death conspiring in her blood
Against the bright truth of her platitude?

III

After the dying, tidying her room,
She pondered, wondered why he had cried out
In protest for his father. Was his shout
Indictment of the seed that filled her womb
Or plea for some known name to mark his tomb?
Now she was parched and hollowed out with doubt.

She had been satisfied the way things were,
Girl among girls, doing the usual things.
Then she had been exalted, hearing wings
Applauding through the galleries of air;
Came to know words that first had made her stare,
And talk to common people as to kings.

123

It never was her doing. She had been
Only the bottle for the conjured wine.
Involved with something magic or divine,
She had no axe to grind, no slate to clean,
Had never bothered with a party line.
Most of the things he said she did not mean.

Now she was empty. The last drop had gone,
And she was her own Mary, uninvolved
With parables or politics, resolved
To self, undedicated, pledged to none.
And just before the colours blurred, dissolved,
She closed the door on her disfigured son.

IV

I am the breath that stirred
Your bells to jubilance;
Conjured from cold distance
As surely as a bird
Immense obeisance:
I am the word.

My irresponsible
Dialogue broke down,
Was hooted, hissed and blown
Off stage in ridicule,
My sad forgiving clown
A love-crossed fool.

But I would blow again
My horn into your sleep;
Herd rational thought like sheep
Into a nursery pen;
Scatter my wolves to sweep
Doubt from the plain.

Yes, I would fill your page,
Your lines with poetry:
With liberating key
Empty the clipped Lark's cage,
And give back wings to free
Ecstatic rage.

Mary, I am cold,
Bare on the brink of mind.
Open, and let me find
A place to grip and hold,
To thrust the exiled seed
In knowing mould.

PADRAIC FIACC (1924-   )

Lives of a Student

At the Feast of the Martyrdom
Of the Innocent
I knelt at the blood-red coverlet
Of the altar and dreamt
Sour morning crimson
Out of a Long Lent

Phallic fern burn
Out of strong skull
Holes for eyes, poppies
And crocuses sprout
Out of the stale dry
Dust of empty soul.

I did not know I could
Not die and be done
With tulip fire in
Worm-raining sun
The roses of the flesh at noon
Leeched on the whittled bone

By virtue of the beautiful
Hungry green fly
That every apple dawn's
Black bitter pit
Would arrow its light into
The eye of once
Young Sebastian.

125

Prayer

The monastery on the mountain
In the cloud is no haven
To take from what I should give
God. I seek no sanctuary from
The island not home
In demon childhood
Nor body by the worm
Bit to rag-worn bone.

Here is no more place to go
From being born
And in between birth more at death.

I pause hurled up on the jaws once were
A green shore of poison in the green
And gasp for breath.

And fly fail climb fall back again
And pay the cost of time I waste and seek
Shelter against the wall
Like the fool Greek
Will bolt in separate directions after all!
O it is all wall and I am weak!

Wait until I am some old wreck
Sowed his wildest oat yet
Then I will want to climb your peak
And lie down on your steep brave bed
And count the rain of hailstones sweet
Hammer on hell from overhead
Free of chains of wings yank feet

Of clay would be safer rooted
In the enough nothing of the day
Chiselling to stone bone
A blur to thin line lands
I tight rope walk on
Any old which way

As with my feet was with my hands
As another one would pray.

Credo Credo
for Aidan and Aine

You soldiers who make for our holy
Pictures, grinding the glass with your
Rifle butts, kicking and jumping on them

With your hob-nailed boots, we
Are a richer dark than the Military
Machine could impose ever.

We have the ancient, hag-ridden, long
In the tooth Mother, with her ugly
Jewish Child

Hangs in the depths of our dark
Secret being, no rifles can reach
Nor bullets, not boots:

It was our icons not our guns
You spat on. When you found our guns
You got down on your knees to them

As if our guns were the holy thing. . .
And even should you shoot the swarthy –
faced Mother with her ugly Jewish Child

Who bleeds with the people, she'll win
Because she loses all with the people,
Has lost every war for centuries with us.

———————————

JEROME KIELY (1925-   )

For a Young Cistercian Monk

He bowed to me when be brought the wine at Mass,
a young monk with an age of graciousness,
    his white robes gesturing eight hundred years of awe,
bowed low, a beetle clawed in humbleness,
    and I must stand erect by splint of canon law.

127

He bowed again before he washed my hands,
his robes like white waves curling for a flat of sands.
　　Worshipful shepherd in a curving crèche
he saw my mask, not me. The Rule's commands
　　hunched him like dolmen to defer to mortal flesh.

I bow to him with all the self I've bent
into these lines; I curtsey to his robe, the tent
　　in which he stores his trackless life; I bow
to his long sleeves, wings of the cormorant
　　that bates with God upon the ebbing tide of now.

I bow to princedom in his circled hair;
I yield to genius in his geometry of prayer,
　　his angled cowl and arc of song at Terce;
I am but knee, he is the holy stair;
　　I bow to him with this obeisance of verse.

Funeral of Paddy Haugh

'That was great weather last week.' Round youth in the earth's eyes.
Look now how the rain draws a spread over the day's twitched face.
'Tough country for walking, this.' Stepping over graves is hard:
the hills are grave mounds over a forgotten Irish race.

When the hearse rolled by high ditches, you saw your own face staring
out of the glass at you walking with Paddy's friends behind.
Sometimes the ragged light wiped out the living faces
and there was only the face of Paddy in the coffin and the mind.

Men spoke as though he had forty times saved hay with them,
but his was no time of fruit but of hopeful burgeoning.
The sun on Tuesday pushed its finger in the sheath of leaves
and death made a glove of Paddy's. He was young and died in the
Spring.

He would have stood on marble, lifted up Christ on His Cross,
but he died in the longing desert, outside the sanctuary.
Yet, the gravediggers mounded an altar of clay, as his life had been,
and God once said, 'Enough to build altar of earth for me.'

He'd not baptise, but water flowed on the coffin's shiny head;
he'd not forgive, but I confessed to him my drab belief;
he'd not anoint, but he prepared a hundred souls for death;
he'd not join two in one, except his mother and his mother's grief.

We stood around his house: it should have been morning in June,
and he should have taken wine in a chalice, and bread, and bent low;
but only rainwater fell into the tarnished chalice of hills
and for bread there was a crust that loosened in the mouth of a crow.

Daffodils by the graveside mastered the wind as they
mastered tomb-earth; they were pennants with 'He rose as He said';
Had you lain on the ground and looked up you'd have seen gilded
    cups tilt
from heaven, as chalices will in Killeen for him who is dead.

What Can a Poet Say?

Always it's winter and my beech tree bare;
    fresh silks of summer are gathered in mouldy sheaves;
the leaves and nuts are falling, and the stares
    rest there a minute, then fall like nuts and leaves.

There is no ark of God where one can place
    what one may hope will be a blossomed rod;
the ark is taken, I am dumb, bowed my face;
    what's left but shout with her who shouted 'Ichabod'?

What ineffectual image may I dare
    put opposite to Mary in her perfect grief –
when the two branch tree was body-bare
    she fell upon Him leaf on twisted leaf?

How could I mock in verse Kinsale my town –
    sickle of sea about the wheaten land,
and all the hills are crippled, bending down
    to see the river take the sickle in its hand?

And Brendan serving Mass – what lens
    gives vision of the baptism in his eyes,
his eyes lake shores of innocence
    or the divinity behind his smile's disguise?

White heather rotting was neglected prayer;
    blue lunging shark was Mary's rise to heaven;
and I sat God in a horizon chair:
    these sins I do confess and shall I be forgiven?

To Mary of the Assumption

O Virgin, on the day you were assumed
music exploded in your silent tomb,
your mushroom of terrible peace grew up the sky
and still the sound waves of your rocketry
ripple in the boom of the midday bells.
Your detonated newness flashes in our prayers,
your radiation falls on Christian souls.

That day you were a kite that floated free:
death's fingers on you numbed and lost their hold.
You made a new astronomy,
you changed the charts, explorer bold,
you not the moon are our chief satellite,
sun of your Son has lit you with His light.

Now you are the tower that men once tried to build
with masonry of pride and trowelled speech
a true skyscraper on the streets above
and men who climb you are a humble guild
and you translate their language into love,
interpreter of God's own Word for each.
No tower of Babel you
but David's Tower.
I am wordfull of you
O mountain and yet flower,
O tongue of the bell in a sky of peace,
O tree of the unforbidden fruit,
O litany of lovely words,
Cliffhouse of the hunted birds,
O star as bright explosively
as splintered sun behind a morning tree.

———————

FRANCIS HARVEY (1925-   )

The Redemptorists of my Youth

They had one-track minds and
declamatory hands; they were
superb actors in a dying or dead
tradition not unaware of
the dramatic impact of a black
biretta flourished above a bowed head.
They strode like soldiers into
embattled pulpits and wore
crucifixes like swords
at their waists. Their invocations were
trumpet calls to battle against
the world, the flesh and the devil
and each flickering candle in our hands was
a faggot lit to burn another heretic. They flushed
sin from the coverts of our souls with
fear and drove God's sacred plover crying
into the upland rain where it remains.

———————————

PEARSE HUTCHINSON (1927-   )

A Tree Absolving

A small cherry in full flower
at a neo-gothic church door
suddenly breaks upon all this
terrible dominical dreariness:
each young man defaced and lost
in that convict garb, sunday best;
each girl's great hair clamped in a hat
shaped like a segment of tinned fruit.
But passing I stopped for a long look
at the tree, and the whole ban broke.

The undeniable elegant spire,
not wounding or climbing the air
as much as resting on it, led
up to the undeniable good:

131

the broad blue sun.
Max Jacob described the sun
as a pagan afraid to come in
to churches, but then the sun
locks no cut fruit in a coy tin.
I stayed out, like sun and tree –
like in that only, in that only –
and suddenly no longer had to try
against such granite odds, the cowed
passion of the sunday crowd,
to feel the earth can be like heaven,
though hell is hallowed once in seven.

Phrases from Isaac of Nineveh

The tears of a man will flow
several times a day.
Then he'll come to continual tears,
and climb toward serenity.
All that is prayer stops,
and the soul prays outside prayer.
When the Spirit dwells in a man,
the man never stops praying,
for the Spirit prays always in him.,
Asleep or awake,
his soul cannot lack prayer.
Eating,
      drinking,
            resting,
                  working,
drowsy:
spontaneous prayer shall perfume his soul.
He'll have no set time for prayer, but be
possessed by it continually.
Even given over
to an appearance of sleep,
prayer secretly invades him.
As a man drest in Christ puts it:
for people in serenity, silence is prayer.
Thoughts in a purified spirit
are like silent voices
praising, in secret, the Invisible.

Knife-Day

for Alan

A man looked up at the blue-and-white sky to say,
below his breath but fiercely:
'If You live, don't let her die
under the knife – whatever you are,
her, or him, or it.'
Then brainwashed-guilty, lowered his head
to glare down
at window-sill, shed, overgrown garden,
withering bicycle – 'if that's where you are' –
down, down, swivelled his glare to where
an hour ago he'd poured chloride of lime
into the corpse of a dustbin alive
with millions – 'Maybe that's where you are,
in one or all of those struggling white worms
struggling in summer joy or against death,
or now still';
but though he clutched the pink wooden
chest-of-drawers top and leaned forward
till his chest met the rim of the tallish
tumbler, his tie got froth,
his nose nearly touched the pane, he couldn't
see the metal carrion on the landing
of the back-door steps, but only
plastic pastel clothes-pegs on a line,
so he'd used up, for now, his abusive imagination,
and couldn't imagine God
as or in
a peg. So he just looked straight ahead
into the summer trees,
at ten or twelve wild roses
in the foreground overgrowing garden
and said: 'Let her go on living.
She deserves to live at least as well as You
deserve to live. She deserves death less.'

RICHARD KELL (1927-   )

A Supplicant Speaks of the Goddess Kwan Yin

She was a human thought, a dainty protest
Against the claims of godhead. We who loved life
And would have looked for truth in songs and flowers,
In wine and precious stones and women's beauty,
We could not take the Master at his word,
Close up the shutters while the sun was climbing
And light the lamp indoors. The wise men gave us paradox;
Some, being frightened by their cleverness,
Locked themselves in for ever and stuffed the windows;
And some allowed themselves a compromise:
Cherished the scents and colours in the garden,
Yet were penitent when they threw a glance
At the slim girls walking in the street.
But we, uncertain of the ways of God,
Too passionate or weak to crush desire,
Or else too much afraid of death (supposing
The wise men were deluded),
We took the risk of sin and prayed for mercy.

Here is the goddess, head graciously tilted,
Gentle and grave and wise, serenely smiling:
So we had come to think of her – a symbol
Of pure mercy. But sometimes I have seen
A little harlot demure and yet coquettish,
Her slender body made for men's hands,
And in the beauty of her brow and eyelids,
The pouting lips, the finger at her breast,
A hint of roguish humour and contempt.
It was as though we knew, in spite of all
Our glossy thoughts, the Master's way was best;
As though our souls betrayed us into truth,
Giving us back our dreams in this carved girl
With the sly face and small ambiguous hand.

Kwan Yin Gives Her Explanation

Sly and satirical you made me
As well as gentle and serene,
Harlot confused with blessed lady

Because the inner mind had seen
The truth you were evading.

Not that the Master's way is right,
But that you are fool and coward –
To have your sensual delight
And still avoid some moral hazard,
Praying when you take fright.

Kill the self-pity you named Kwan Yin,
Then call me lover instead of whore
And joyfully reinterpret sin.
Or smash my image, dance no more
And light the lamp within.

Sabbath Triptych

Music by Wagner: horns and violins
propose the condonation of his sins
who honoured God the Logos. Mr Smith
would rather have a car to tinker with,
a hedge to trim, and God the Mechanist –
aloof, the cosmos ticking on his wrist.
Between the radio and electric shears,
myself and two Jehovah's Witnesses
contending on the doorstep. 'It's all here
in black and white, the prophecies are clear'
they tell me, shaking dust off, snapping God
the Father in a briefcase. Overhead
the unclouded sunlight equally surveys
its colours redisposed a thousand ways.

Deficient Cause

So *you* began the violence, the pain –
    with you the whole creation fell!
Your father saved the progeny of Seth
    and cursed the tribe of Cain.
The lion tore the heart from the gazelle
    and children starved to death.

Your sin was certainly original!
  Even Augustine, who believed
nothingness made you love the lesser good,
  was baffled by the Fall.
If you transgressed your nature, you achieved
  more than Jehovah could.

Making you perfect man he made you free –
  though what alternative you had
to choosing rightly, since your will was true,
  is difficult to see.
If something ('nothing'?) turned your good will bad,
  that wasn't willed by you.

Poor Adam. What the fossil record pleads,
  kinship is quick to grant. You learned,
as surely as the protozoic slime,
  to satisfy your needs.
That 'disobedience' was a fire that burned
  aeons before your time.

Walking with Matron

In the Nilgiris, a platoon of Christ's cadets
with uniform shirts and topee helmets, we were
marched under tropical leaves by Matron, singing
'Stand up, stand up for Jesus'. She led us firmly
out of the hooting shadows to revelations
of sky and mountain, precipices with slow white
ropes of water dropping three thousand feet to the
empty plain, and we rested there in the silence
that calmed her voice as she told us about the one
sheep that was lost and found. We filled our handkerchiefs
with tea berries, put beetles like gems in boxes
velveted with moss. On the way back I managed
not to crunch my peppermint: it dissolved on my
tongue like a sliver of ice, and my bitten mouth
was cool and peaceful. But near the school we halted,
while Matron lifted her walking-stick and battered
a small brown snake to death, her spectacles glowing.

The Dancers

*'These more aesthetic forms of experience
must be carefully distinguished from those
which indubitably involve a change of
one's nature.'*

Carl Jung

I

First light, faint and cool,
graces the sleeping village.
At low tide, alone,
I watch the gulls
bathe with a slap of wings
in the freshet sliding
into the salt shallows of the harbour.

How long since the missionaries brought
holy baptism here to sweeten
the bitter soul? Today the unbelievers
come for holiday healing: cars
glut the small streets that wind
uphill to where the Wesleyan chapel stands.

The place is deserted now
except for the splashing gulls
and me, with the taint
of fear and lassitude in my blood,
thinking of this and of things
the Methodist preachers blazed
for good or ill: how often did belief
in the need for grace and cleansing
make bitter the sweet soul?

In a cottage parlour where
I crossed out words and phrases
hangs a sampler stitched
a hundred years ago by a teenage girl:
two evangelical stanzas, then
'The serpent beguilèd me and I did eat'.
Remembering now, I drop this irony into
a chaos that the mind,
intent on wholeness, naturally –

shaping some argument about
my craft, my father's mission, and the Word –
has started to inform.

II

On the island rock standing
offshore like a crust of jet
in foils of running silver,
St Clement lived – whether
scared into uneasy quietude,
scouring his soul with the rough wind
for his redemption only, or becoming
a radiant centre to relay the Word,
who knows? Some believe in
holy emanations, as though a grace
could flow from his praying spirit
into the light and air
and the sea's voice, to stream across
the harbour and through the village,
seasoning with a subtle immanence
the grain of human life.

But Gautama returned to make
words out of the Word, obscure codings
for luminous apprehensions;
Francis danced his joy
before the cardinals, preached
love to citizens and to sparrows;
and Wesley, who had written once
'a quarter before nine I felt my heart
strangely warmed', went out on horseback
to win the mining towns.
Eighty years after, Billy Bray of Truro,
husband and profligate, who prayed
in desperation through
a six-day hell, knew
the moment his life changed, and brought
his tidings gladly to the market place.

III

In Cornwall, dreaming men
could stride into sweet nests
of fern and heather, whispering hollows,

138

and drop two thousand feet
through a howling blackness.
Peering in, we lobbed
a ball of rock, and waited.
Three times we heard it thud,
the note changing, diminishing, until
its plumb fall into pinpoint depth
stunned from the earth's drum
in a far-off echoing dark
the last word: *doom*.

Their faces deathly under candle flames,
fingers grappling rungs, boots tapping,
they journey down into
a trapped asphyxiating night,
to bear the pick's shock
at the level's end hour after hour,
hugged by the stale heat, the haze of filth
fastening on skin and lungs.

The will has grown
tough as the body, turned wretchedness to
enduring, till a man can love
the rich rock he curses, his dry spirit
pause for a draught of sympathy or praise.
But not the reprobate
who made them roar with laughter
a week ago: his lips,
famous for their speeding
of beer and blasphemous wit,
mutter remotely now, his stare
takes root in an inward vision.
The hardness he cracks open –
by turns listless, frenzied –
is more than the earth's bone,
his labour more
than the day's wage will token.

Fear of flood and rockfall,
of missed footings, the drop
to annihilation – this they had learned
to tolerate through the long sober stints,

to escape from in the dissolutions
of drunkenness and lust.
Hell was familiar, finite, tangible,
until the preachers came
transforming, amid tears and hallelujahs,
fact into symbol, known torments into
the unimaginable horrors of perdition.

Billy Bray, his will strung tight,
lives one rung at a time, drags upward
the dead weight of existence; sweating, feels
the tug of uncanny air,
and hears the pit breathe
Let go, fall, finish. . .
but glancing up, and seeing
the blackness pricked with daylight,
prays, hardens his grip,
and climbs again in the soft candleshine
he wears upon his brow.

IV

Alone on the sixth day, lost
in the nightstorm of his mind, he turns
to the first and simplest act, the firm
reality of touch; the Word,
cradled in miner's hands,
opening like bread broken, like split rock,
reveals the buried light of his salvation:
Ask, and it shall be given you;
seek, and ye shall find;
knock, and it shall be opened unto you.

Perfect in faith now, his prayer deep,
he moves from sorrow into the dancing
stillness of the Word beyond words,
and filled with amazing love, his spirit
clean and light, opens the cottage door
on a place he never lived in: 'I remember
this, that everything looked
new to me – the people,
the fields, the cattle, the trees. I was like
a man in a new world.'

Unearthly transformations – letting in,
deeper than all theologies,
the love that casts out fear!
Some say the will becomes
pure prism – or a jewel
hoarding a little daylight still
in obdurate particles, while the rest
is medium for epiphanies of colour.

Monstrous when the soul gorges on
the entire spectrum, and black opacity
declares itself translucent.
Better recluse then, or it will shape
the world with fire and rack,
needle and gas, proceeding like Der Führer
'with all the assurance of a somnambulist
where Providence dictates'.

These others tantalize, made whole by love
(the heart 'strangely warmed') yet so exacting
their disciplines could warp
lives that had trembled in the storms
of their great sermons. Wesley's rule
expelled 'disorderly walkers' from the classes:
and what was their desperate end – dropping
through fear's black shafts –
whom grace never shocked into the sober
euphoria of the saved.

And Billy Bray? About intolerance –
except to note a brief
offensive on the vanity of beards –
biography is silent. For the rest,
it seems he stopped drinking once and for all;
in meetings he would dance and shout
for pure joy; his wit was a bright knife
shredding the devil's arguments, his prayers
worked miracles of healing.

The truth was poorer, maybe.
Yet something happened: no legend
grows from history without
a living root to grow from.

Something was reached, released:
underground water
rising pure in the parched well –
love by its own pressure
casting out emptiness.

Logos, Atman, Tao. . . words,
no longer needed when their definitions
fade in the sudden brilliance of their meaning.
'A poor spectacle,' said Billy Bray,
'to have only the telling part of the love of Christ:
it is the feeling part that makes us happy.'
Something happened. Suppose a man, seeking,
found his humanity, became
his Self so instantly
through a paroxysm of fearful longing
it seemed a miracle, but was
the shaft striking water that's always there.

V

May they rest in peace,
Clement and Billy Bray.
Although I feel
the need they must have felt,
I am past expecting
wonderful changes now.
A fear like theirs
is storm in the night sky,
ours a cold fret
blearing the roads, reducing vision:
few are scared enough to become saints.
And should I find
some credible affirmation of the Word,
it won't be in their doctrines.

Go down into the depths of history, through
the creeds and the persecutions:
Mahatma Gandhi, peacemaker,
dies from a gunshot on his way to prayers;
George Fox lies ill in the jailhouse;
undying candle, Latimer's body kindles;
Jesus bleeds on the crux of life and death.
Over and over, taking

the preacher's myth for fact,
men got the meaning wrong.
Yet all may have possessed it:
what clear-headed Anaxagoras,
jailed for impiety, tried to formulate,
the people, unsuspecting, found perhaps
in songs, dances, delicate bowls, buildings,
communities bound by justice or by love:
what we might witness here in the lineaments
of rock and water, harbour and winding street.

The rising sun gilds
hermit's isle and preacher's chapel;
glancing from waves, dazzles me where I stand
above the turning tide.
And air that breathed on water
fills my blood, bringing
to every informed cell
in the body's universe
a slow sustaining fire.

Such things are natural.
And here too, where thought and feeling
haunt the flesh (though strangely beyond space),
the elements dance, a subtle
agency weaves a logic.
I call this faith of a kind:
to see in art
the nature of the mind,
and to suppose it shapes
from chaos, from the absurd,
a structured wholeness that implies the Word.

———————————

RICHARD MURPHY (1927-   )

Largesse

There's a trawler at the quay landing fish.
Could it be one of the island boats?
Seldom we see them, but how glad we are.

They have a generous custom
Of giving away a box of dabs or fluke,
For luck, of course, for the unlucky poor.

And this is how it works:
Three tramps are walking down the docks
Casually, not hurrying, getting there
With enough drinking time to spare,
When a blue car fins along
And sharks the free fish-box.

Usually at this dusky hour
That car's owner
Is kneeling in the parlour with his wife.
If you go into their shop you hear
Nine decades of the rosary
And a prayer for Biafra.

THOMAS KINSELLA (1928-   )

The Monk

He tramped in the fading light
Of a late February day
Between hedges stiff with the wind.
Rough folds of his robe swung.
His boots trod stone and clay.
His blown habit crouched
In the wet daylight's decay.
A spade across his shoulder
Slanted into the sky.
Sunk in the cowl his quiet eye.

A sense of scrubbed flesh in the path;
A thought of washing in cold hours
When dreams are scrubbed off
In a chill room, huge flowers,
Night blooms, accidentally plucked,
Each dawn devours;

Of a haggard taste in the mouth
Savouring in death a tide of light,
Harvest in all decay,
Spring in February night.

Faith

An Old Atheist Pauses by the Sea

I choose at random, knowing less and less.
The shambles of the seashore at my feet
Yields a weathered spiral: I confess
– Appalled at how the waves have polished it –
I know that shores are eaten, rocks are split,
Shells ghosted. Something hates unevenness.
The skin turns porcelain, the nerves retreat
And then the will, and then the consciousness.

Into Thy Hands

Diver, noting lightly how the board
Gives to the body, now with like intent
I watch the body give to the instant, seeing
In risk a salty joy: let accident
Complete our dreadful journey into being.

Here, possessed of time and flesh at last,
I hurl the Present bodily at the Past:
Outstretched, into the azure chasm he soared.

A Pillar of the Community

Descending on Merchants' Alley, Lucifer
Gave jet-black evidence of fatherhood.
A column rose to meet him from the mud;
He perched and turned to metal. Polished, foursquare,
A noble savage stopped in stride, he stood.
Now gingerly our honest deals are done
Under that puckish rump, inscribed: Do good.
Some care and a simple faith will get you on.

Carol

Garden and gardener He made
And then for seed Himself He laid
　　To rectify our loss.
O red the Spring on the cruel blade
And lily-white His body splayed
　　In pity on the cross.

Haunting our harvest like a thief
He hides His flesh in every sheaf,
　　His blood in every fruit,
But rank the weed – Our Saviour's Grief –
We nourish into thorns and leaf
　　To live by the sour root.

His is the hunger of the pyre
The seasons wither on; admire
　　His great and ghostly paces
About the fume of His desire –
How many souls retreat, retire,
　　And turn away their faces!

Meadows whiten, stores are piled.
Again in our icy barn the Child
　　Sleeps before the play.
Adore Him, now our hearts are mild,
To profit us when we have whiled
　　Our innocence away.

Office for the Dead

The grief-chewers enter, their shoes hard on the marble,
In white lace and black skirts, books held to their loins.
A silver pot tosses in its chains as they assemble
About the coffin, heavy under its cloth, and begin.

Back and forth, each side in nasal unison
Against the other, their voices grind across her body.
We watch, kneeling like children, and shrink as their Church
Latin chews our different losses into one.

– All but certain images of her pain that will not,
In the coarse process, pass through the cloth and hidden boards
To their peace in the shroud; that delay, still real –

High thin shoulders – eyes boring out of the dusk –
Wistful misshapenness – a stripped, dazzling mouth –
Her frown as she takes the candle pushed into her hands
In the last crisis, propped up, dying with worry.

Sanctus. We listen with bowed heads to the thrash of chains
Measuring the silence. The pot gasps in its smoke.
An animal of metal dragging itself and breathing. . .

JOHN MONTAGUE (1929-   )

A Footnote on Monasticism:
Dingle Peninsula

In certain places, still, surprisingly, you come
Upon them, resting like old straw hats set down
Beside the sea, weather-beaten but enduring
For a dozen centuries; here the mound
That was the roof has slithered in
And the outlines you can barely trace:
Nor does it matter since every wilderness
Along this coast retains more signs
In ragged groupings of these cells and caves
Of where the hermits, fiercely dispossessed,
Found refuge among gulls and rocks
The incessant prayer of nearby waves.

Among darkening rocks he prayed,
Body chastened and absurd,
An earth-bound dragging space
His spirit blundered like a bird:
Hands, specialised by prayer,
Like uplifted chalices,
Nightly proffering the self
To soundless, perfect messengers.

147

There are times, certainly, looking through a window
At amiable clustered humanity, or scanning
The leaves of some old book, that one might wish
To join their number, start a new and fashionable
Sect beside the Celtic sea, long favourable
To dreams and dreamers; anchorites whose love
Was selfishly alone, a matter so great
That only to stone could they whisper it:
Breaking the obstinate structure of flesh
With routine of vigil and fast,
Till water-cress stirred on the palate
Like the movement of a ghost.

In ceaseless labour of the spirit,
Isolate, unblessed;
Until quietude of the senses
Announces presence of a guest;
Desolation final,
Rock within and rock without
Till from the stubborn rock of the heart
The purifying waters spurt.

RICHARD WEBER (1932-   )

The Priest in the Train

Turns over the brief chapters of his breviary,
His mind's light afloat on God's lonely silence.
His pale face fervent with faith in faith,
God is my god, his white fingers say,
Whispering among the leaves of his sacred book.
His thighs curve over his crossed sex
(That second master) negated by designed neglect,
Unfree for love in a world of free love.
His coal black, polished shoes suggest a little
The archetypal, world deflecting devil's hoof,
But only, perhaps, by the contrary contraries
Of a lax layman's faithless turn of thought.
Yet is it scent of incense or smell of hellfire
That lingers after this nameless one's departure,
Tall, solitary and ascetic, at Golder's Green?

JAMES SIMMONS (1933-   )

Eden

He threw them out and slammed the gate shut
for what He found them up to. He was scared
like all angry people and unprepared
for love. He decided to blame it on 'that slut'.

Morally hung over He walked the walls,
straightened His stone picnic-tables, stared
sickly at the new padlock and the guard's sword,
waiting to welcome repentant prodigals.

If only they'd argue, face to face; but no.
They sneaked back to pick up a radio
left in a secret place in the undergrowth,
aimlessness their element they were loath
to risk losing. They drifted into the night,
relieved in every way to travel light.
The unprejudiced world was what those two lacked,
and of course they avoided the huge pathetic back
of God. To this day He is standing there,
banished. There *was* a world elsewhere.

———————————

JAMES LIDDY (1934-   )

Lady Day, Arklow

Summer another bower for us who if really alive
Would become sensualists with good manners
    I decide
On the Church steps. August the gay painter
    Of the dahlias

In the Canon's garden. Between the cinema
    And hotel
White dots along the meadows of Sheepwalk. . .
The baptised do not see through stained glass
   Forever blind.

149

Yet, Lady, it is good to keep the candles
      Burning
And the tale of love repeated in a low
      Foreign speech
To hear the favour asked at the wedding.

To travel the dusty roads of your first born
And finish weeping at the foot of the cross
      Though you remain
At Ephesus and the dead Lord continues as
      A message – like art.

Pacem in Terris

A seemingly Christless world in the eyes of the pharisees
the idyllic socialist state without inequalities
a few of us in our wish for man dream about. . .
for gombeen Ireland as elsewhere. . .

I, backroom chanter of the poor, think of
the love bread the gay Jew left us:
I see from the crumbs how the employees the weak
of feudal lands can not inherit without God;

He (the worker) will bless any proletarian dawn
on the beaches and farms or in the solitude of seas,
will be present in the tearwiping comradely love
the shared work the birth-death details,

If this new society comes there will be many churches
packed like harvest barns and apostolic priests,
our holy mother the Catholic Church
the lily planted in a better field. . .

married ideologies where we meet. . .
the religion of Lenin that of Christ and the poets;
with Eluard I acknowledge brotherhood destroys death
with Neruda I find the poet's begging bowl.

                                                    1963

150

DESMOND O'GRADY (1935-   )

Was I Supposed to Know?

When,
In a blue-sharp, fallow sky,
With wind in hair
And grey of rock, angled by ages, sharpening the eye,
I
Stamped down that cut stone stair
Towards sand and sea
And clawed, nails scratching, down from deaf-mute cliffs to where
Were tracks and trees below –
Was I supposed to know?

When,
With senses quick as compass
And tightened skin,
In breaking clearing, fell on Church and Churchyard moss
I,
Helpless, toeheeled in
To Christ and Cross
And, staring staring silence, felt small as a pin,
Felt schoolboy years ago –
Was I supposed to know?

Was I supposed to know
That
Each fisted flex of heart
And wide of eye,
Each patch of thought in bone-sprung skull; each stutter start
Of unravelled blood in my
Knit flesh and bone;
And every studied part I cast me as a boy;
That all my rebel scorn
And mock at prayer,
My every bedded bitch and spilled out kids unborn,
Were
All marked mine with care –
By some high Law
Or some high guiding Plan – to lead me back to where,
Again,

151

With coffin smell of pew
And criss of Cross,
Unwinking eyes of saints and hushed confession queue –
For one loud nervous boot
Of frightened heart,
I felt the Churchyard fidget fear of schooltied youth?

The Flesh and the Spirit

Beyond the monastery: meadows, woods,
the stream and the sun setting in summer.
Light and shadow in the cloister. Light
through stained glass on stone walls.
No decoration but an amber radiance
round a darkening sanctuary.
Rise and fall of the chant
at the day's declining
Salve Regina, Mater Misericordiae...
And the devotion!

Capitulation of the stubborn spirit;
peace with the land, the light of the sun,
the watching, unanswering statues?
Was that what we worshipped? The statues?
Or was it the amber radiance?
We needed no more: capitulation
of the spirit; the chant's swell at day's end:
vita dulcedo et spes nostra salve...

It phrased an answer for some of us
and some stayed. The rest
went our various ways –
some never to be seen again; some
in search of reputation; some to continue
the ways of their forefathers. At times,
in distant places, I'm reminded
of all of us;
of our devotion;
of the unanswering statues.

JAMES McAULEY (1936-)

The Passion

In 1964 a French film unit brought back from Kivu Province in the Congo a sequence in a village which had been recaptured from rebel forces. Among many instances of brutality during the 'questioning' of the villagers, the film showed one young man, bound hand and foot, being kicked to death by the government soldiery.

And before the dutiful soldiers came up to Gethsemane
Christ wept and asked his father to forego the trial,
Then said, 'Not my will but thine. . .'
                                        There's little enmity
About these soldiers as they smile and smoke

And nonchalantly kick at the closed eyes: their style
Grows out of every soldier's duty while they poke
At the writhing loins till they are still, and while
Their sergeant waves at the camera, and while they spit

Carelessly into the dust around the matted hair.
                                            Christ spoke
Of love from his cross, but I cannot fit
Golgotha's theme to the savage sermon evoked
By the sergeant shrugging, by the pistol shot to the head,

By the turning away of the soldiers, by the grit
From the street that dries the quiet blood.
                                        If Christ is dead,
Has he not yet risen? Or is this on the screen a skit,
A playful allegory from history's frivolous masque,

A killing as gratuitous as that in which Christ bled
To redeem this sin? Is it his father I should ask
Why this should earn for soldiers their daily bread?
What is his mercy? Should I condone the soldiers' smiling too?

That villager's bound heels and wrists have something to do,
God, with the reason I do not believe in You.

———————

The Smell

The inside of the church absorbed the rain's thunder,
Lightning deceived and killed, the thunder never lied,
The thunder knelt and prayed at the high altar.
I was six years old. I knelt and prayed at her side.

She was a woman in black, she of the white head,
She whose lips rivalled the lips of the rain.
Someone closer to her than anyone had died far back.
That was the story. The story created her pain.

Out of her pain she prayed, always on her knees,
Her lips shaped secrets like rain in August grass.
Her white head, I knew, could not betray or deceive,
The thunder imitated the secrets of her heart.

I knelt at her side, my shoulder brushing her black,
Her lips surrendered visions of her private heaven and hell.
Drugged by her whispers, my head sank into her side,
My body and soul, in that instant, entered her smell,

Not merely the smell of her skin, but the smell
Of her prayers and pain, the smell of her long loss,
The smell of the years that had whitened her head,
That made her whisper to the pallid Christ on his cross,

The rent, dumb Christ, listener at the doors of the heart,
The pummelled Christ, the sea of human pain,
The sated Christ, the drinker of horrors,
The prisoner Christ, dungeoned in flesh and bone.

Her smell opened her locked world,
My closed eyes saw something of mine,
My small world swam in her infinite world
And did not drown but rose where the sun shone

On silence following the thunder's majestic prayer
For all the pain of all the living and dead,
I opened my eyes to the silence
Blessing her black clothes, her white head,

Blessing the smell that had told me something
Beyond lips' whispers and heart's prayer.
She took my hand in her hand, we moved together
Out of the church into the rain-cleaned air.

SEAMUS HEANEY (1939-   )

Docker

There, in the corner, staring at his drink,
The cap juts like a gantry's crossbeam,
Cowling plated forehead and sledgehead jaw.
Speech is clamped in the lips' vice.

That fist would drop a hammer on a Catholic –
Oh yes, that kind of thing could start again;
The only Roman collar he tolerates
Smiles all round his sleek pint of porter.

Mosaic imperatives bang home like rivets;
God is a foreman with certain definite views
Who orders life in shifts of work and leisure.
A factory horn will blare the Resurrection.

He sits, strong and blunt as a Celtic cross,
Clearly used to silence and an armchair:
Tonight the wife and children will be quiet
At slammed door and smoker's cough in the hall.

Poor Women in a City Church

The small wax candles melt to light,
Flicker in marble, reflect bright
Asterisks on brass candlesticks
At the Virgin's altar on the right
Blue flames are jerking on wicks.

Old dough-faced women with black shawls
Drawn down tight kneel in the stalls.
Cold yellow candle-tongues, blue flame

155

Mince and caper as whispered calls
Take wing up to the Holy Name.

Thus each day in the sacred place
They kneel. Golden shrines, altar lace,
Marble columns and cool shadows
Still them. In the gloom you cannot trace
A wrinkle on their beeswax brows.

In Gallarus Oratory

You can still feel the community pack
This place: it's like going into a turfstack,
A core of old dark walled up with a stone
A yard thick. When you're in it alone
You might have dropped, a reduced creature
To the heart of the globe. No worshipper
Would leap up to his God off this floor.

Founded there like heroes in a barrow
They sought themselves in the eye of their King
Under the black weight of their own breathing,
And how he smiled on them as out they came,
The sea a censer, and the grass a flame.

The Other Side

I
Thigh-deep in sedge and marigolds
a neighbour laid his shadow
on the stream, vouching

'It's poor as Lazarus, that ground,'
and brushed away
among the shaken leafage;

I lay where his lea sloped
to meet our fallow,
nested on moss and rushes,

my ear swallowing
his fabulous, biblical dismissal,
that tongue of chosen people.

When he would stand like that
on the other side, white-haired,
swinging his blackthorn

at the marsh weeds,
he prophesied above our scraggy acres,
then turned away

towards his promised furrows
on the hill, a wake of pollen
drifting to our bank, next season's tares.

II

For days we would rehearse
each patriarchal dictum;
Lazarus, the Pharoah, Solomon

and David and Goliath rolled
magnificently, like loads of hay
too big for our small lanes,

or faltered on a rut –
'Your side of the house, I believe,
hardly rule by the book at all.'

His brain was a whitewashed kitchen
hung with texts, swept tidy
as the body o' the kirk.

III

Then sometimes when the rosary was dragging
mournfully on in the kitchen
we would hear his step round the gable

though not until after the litany
would the knock come to the door
and the casual whistle strike up

on the doorstep, 'A right-looking night,'
he might say, 'I was dandering by
and says I, I might as well call.'

But now I stand behind him
in the dark yard, in the moan of prayers.
He puts a hand in a pocket

or taps a little tune with the blackthorn
shyly, as if he were party to
lovemaking or a stranger's weeping.

Should I slip away, I wonder,
or go up and touch his shoulder
and talk about the weather

or the price of grass-seed?

In Illo Tempore

The big missal splayed
and dangled silky ribbons
of emerald and purple and watery white.

Intransitively we would assist,
confess, receive. The verbs
assumed us. We adored.

And we lifted our eyes to the nouns.
Altar stone was dawn and monstrance noon,
the word rubric itself a bloodshot sunset.

Now I live by a famous strand
where seabirds cry in the small hours
like incredible souls

and even the range wall of the promenade
that I press down on for conviction
hardly tempts me to credit it.

SEAMUS DEANE (1940-)

Epiphany

Sounds playing truant from their bell
Faded around us as we trudged to Mass
Through a swarming, an inebriate snow.
The steeple of slamming iron let fall
Delicate ikons of tinkling glass

Which altar-boys shook out again like foil
At consecration. The stations of the cross,
Plastered in fourteen friezes on the walls,
Kept their fixed profiles on the full-faced crib
While our heads bowed before the stall

Where Christ took up his five-point-star career
From small beginnings. Just a month before
We had untuned his sky with a blaring siren
And run to the stinking air-raid shelter.
But nothing came. Fooled by false alarmings,

We yet concede nothing. Christ hung,
A phantom sound whose rumoured birth
Brought hundreds a Roman and unjust desert.
Perhaps fake sirens and clear Christmas bells
Bring all to such shelters where the smells

Of gas and incense freely mingle
To give us expectation. Piety and rage
Change their ratios with age.
Childhood and perfumes of a holy day
Recall our future each Epiphany.

DEREK MAHON (1941-)

Nostalgias

The chair squeaks in a high wind,
Rain falls from its branches,
The kettle yearns for the

159

Mountain, the soap for the sea.
In a tiny stone church
On the desolate headland
A lost tribe is singing 'Abide With Me'.

MICHAEL HARTNETT (1941-   )

The Lord Taketh Away

In virgin cloisters from fourteen
It was taught as the only life:
Before the body made its moves
The best wife was the spiritual wife.

They preached the convent was the bar
Between the wanted and the wild
And poured their holy lies upon
The immaculate logic of this child.

For her I wrote impotent songs,
Transparent and slight as tears,
And offered her mortal happiness
For some unspecified years.

Because for her death was
The consequence of a kiss,
While Christ, as ghostly husband,
Offered immortal bliss.

I fought, that devious lessons
Might somehow be undone,
But the odds were three to one:
Father and Son and Holy Ghost.
I had no chance against such a host.

Mrs Halpin and the Lightning

When thunder entered like an easter priest
and draped its purple on Mullach a' Radhairc
a horse took fright and broke its neck
against a pierstone:

the carshafts gave like small bones
and the tilted wheel spun.
When the blule sheets crackled
with electric starch
Mrs Halpin with a goose's wing
flailed holy water drops
like the steel tips of holy whips
to beat the demons from the room.
But they would not go away.
Their garments shook her rosary
as they danced on the stone floor.
Her fear was not the simple fear of one
who does not know the source of thunder:
these were the ancient Irish gods
she had deserted for the sake of Christ.
They waited in the earth and sky
to punish and destroy
their fickle congregation.
Mrs Halpin knew the reason why.

(Mullach a' Radhairc: hills to the south-west of Newcastle West)

JOHN F DEANE (1943-   )

Matins

We walked round shrubbery, cowled in silence,
somewhere in the long pause of mid-morning;
the fuchsia hung in scarlet, bees drew out
their honey; high trees benignly watched, long
used to circling figures on the gravel; we
read Rodriguez, his tome of hugh wonders, deeds
of saints, glories of holiness, miracles
sprouting out of deserts. Secretly, I longed
that those naked whores spirited out of hell
into the monks' cells should tempt me, too;
I fasted, prayed, scaled the cliffs of sanctity
to no avail; always the sudden wren
distracted, a weed's unexpected beauty on a stone,
coolness of peas bursting against my palette; I
stayed in my tiny group, going round and round.

Penance

They leave their shoes, like signatures, below;
above, their God is waiting. Slowly they rise
along the mountainside where rains and winds go
hissing, slithering across. They are hauling up

the bits and pieces of their lives, infractions
of the petty laws, the little trespasses and
sad transgressions. But this bulked mountain
is not disturbed by their passing, by this mere

trafficking of shale, shifting of its smaller stones.
When they come down, feet blistered, and sins
fretted away, their guilt remains, and that black
mountain stands against darkness above them.

The Great Skellig

Was this, God's city, the pleroma?

souls pitched along the cliffs
fledgling elect?

everywhere sheer rock,
miracle gardens in crevices, the white
gannets moving over the waters
silent, like spirits;

such contact with the naked Christ,
with the Trinity
of stone and air and water, bred
certainties.

Now, while storms come scourging
the trees outside, and a solitary
heron curses at the cold, I sit
by the fire's warmth, imagining
reincarnations, and a strong
habited figure in my bones' cell
cries out in his despair.

Francis of Assisi

1182 - 1982

Summer has settled in again; ships,
softened to clouds, hang on the horizon;
buttercups, like bubbles, float
on fields of a silver-grey haze; and words
recur, such as light, the sea, and God

the frenzy of crowds jostling towards the sun
contains silence, as eyes contain
blindness;
      we say, may the Lord
turning his face towards you
give you peace

morning and afternoon the cars moved out
onto the beach and clustered, shimmering,
as silver herring do in a raised net; this
is a raucous canticle to the sun

altissimu, omnipotente, bon Signore. . .

to set up flesh
in images of snow and of white
roses, to preach to the sea
on silence, to man
on love, is to strain towards death
as towards a body without flaw

our poems too, are gestures of a faith
that words of an undying love
may not be without some substance

words hovered like larks about his head, dropped
like blood from his ruptured hands

tue so' le laude et onne benedictione. . .

we play, like children, awed and hesitant
at the ocean's edge;
between dusk and dark the sea

as if it were God's long and reaching fingers
appropriates each footprint from the sand

I write down words, such as light, the sea, and God
and a bell rides out across the fields
like a man on a horse with helmet and lance
gesturing foolishly towards night

laudato si, Signore, per sora nostra morte corporale

at night, the cars project
ballets of brightness and shadow on the trees
and pass, pursuing
darkness at the end of their tunnels of light

the restful voices have been swept by time
beyond that storybook night sky
where silence
drowns them out totally

Monasterboice

Buite climbed from here to Heaven
on a ladder held by angels; when he came
down, they cowled him, that bright
eye, that melodious voice; but his words
hang about God's settlement, among tourists
rare as wasps in the September heat
and nettle-clumps about to yield
their cache of rubble.

The stone tower, too still points to Heaven
like an arm broken off at the wrist; there are
echoes of handbells urging to lauds, and steep
steps rising through its sexless dark.

Muiredach's wondrous cross
weighs on the earth to hold it down; here
the risen Christ has made
Satan his footstool, and God's
strictures, chiselled on stone, fade
like memories; fingers braille
whimsical and interlacing snakes, to learn
only the neutral presences of stone.

The base of the cross, nude
after the winds of centuries, enters
the earth; there is sign of crab and goat,
the repressed roar of bull and ram; and when a young
girl stumbled and fell down the ledged
shaft of the tower, her scream
was an echo of the dark invaders' years.

PADRAIG J DALY (1943-   )

Sagart 1

In many ways you're like an old man. Perhaps
You walk alone more than most people twice your age.
You notice each change of weather, the drift
Of smoke to sky. There is a certain decorum
You follow in your dress, the way you comb your hair.

You may have many acquaintances, few friends;
Besides your unreplying God you have no confidant.
Nevertheless you lift your hat to all. Old ladies
Especially will seek you out, sometimes a sinner.
You are guest at many celebrations, a must at birth or death.

Sometimes you wonder whether this is how God intended it.

Sagart 3

Like old countrywomen
By fireplaces on Winter evenings
We sit alone.

Outside day draws in; dogs
Bark to one another across acres
Of mountain; the last red hen
Goes wearily to shelter; younger
Voices rise and fall in laughter
Or argument; there is banging of churns
And milk poured quietly.

We have some urgent tale to tell
About life; but our mouths open
And no sound gathers shape.
We belong out by the side of things.

Problem

I understand Francis – all the stuff about the birds,
Throwing his clothes at his father; the singing, praising Heart.

Once I travelled from Rome into Umbria
To his town, his green mountains,
His fast streams,

Saw the coarse cloth he wore against cold,
The chapel shrining Chiara's hair.

Teresa Sanchez was never a problem:
In convent or covered wagon
In constant seesaw up and down towards God.

Or John
Soaring through his bars like a linnet in song.

But I am blind still to the Jew
My life traipses after;

And the spacelessness of God
Hesitates the hand I reach
Behind cross and tabernacle

Into his paltry loneliness.

Augustine: Letter to God

I
Where praise is impossible
I will praise;
And sing where sound faces silence.

I carry death about in me
And inevitable
Cold;

Yet I will sing
Or, failing,
Burst asunder with love.

II

Man cannot evade You:
Every wary mouse,
The ant that builds and climbs,

Each small limpet on a rock,
The waters sucked noisily
Through stones on the shore,

The sleek and watery cormorant
Compel him
To shout You out.

He is the phosphorous sea
Stirred to consciousness,
The cold gravels of the underbed.

From the acids of first time,
From the tepid waters of creation
He draws his voice;

And all creation
Beating at his flesh and pores,
Binds him to praise.

And all creation –
Hills rising out of him
Into sudden seas,

Black shoreline,
The ocean's grit –
Binds him inescapably to praise.

And nowhere but in praise
Can quark or atom
Or any fraction else of mass

Find peace.

III

Each flower
Requires knowledge

And the raindrops
On the curlew's wing

Fall
As questions.

There is a curiosity
In every piece of burnt wood.

IV

What am I
That You require me?

And what is my house
That You should come to it?

And what my love that
You demand my loving

And I am lost
Unless I reach and love?

V

I call:
And You are already in my voice.

I stretch:
And You are trembling at my fingertips.

You are here and smiling
While I send invitations out.

I draw circles to contain You,
Make clay jars:

But You are
Circle and jar

And the space within
And the space without

And the spacelessness
Without the final space,

Place
Where place has no meaning,

Time
Where all is an endless now.

I call
And I am my own answer;

I stretch
Only to where I have started.

Encounter

Monotony of sun
On sand and scrub,
A place of wild beasts
And long shadows.

At last he comes
To green and olivegroves,
Vineyards,
Houses climbing beyond walls
Along a hillside.

Here the tempter waits,
Full of candour,
Offering for easy sale
All the green kingdoms of the world.

And he,
Though gaunt from fasting,
Needing rest,

Some perfect star
Seen a lifetime back
Determining him,

Passes slowly by.

JOHN ENNIS (1944-   )

Miserere

Students tiered in the choir
Spring us Allegri's Miserere

Harmony unfolds its wings
Ecce parvus, ecce avis

We watch its flight
Flutter to rooflight

Out, up sky there's elevation
Blue infrangible heaven;

Yet treble taut notes kite
Cry buoyant as if eternally

Beat at the sun-shafted dome
One with all flesh, feather and bone

I remember Rogation Days,
Walking in the dawn,

Crocus by rivulet and snowdrops
Grew. God was approachable.

Love, hide your streaming face, facade,
Sing. Walk. Surpliced two by two.

Mourne glitters ice white
Still in the sunlight.

All that glisters on the Altar
Is gold I cared for.

Go instruct the flowers
Time is on our side. Snow
                    showers.

Treble, bird proves it is no dream
Though no god drinks from our undine stream.

PAUL DURCAN (1944-   )

The Seminary

High up above the town on a spur of rock
Towers the seminary
Which once was our small town's dormant volcano
And source of trade
But now the seminarians are detaching themselves from it like lava
And our fathers and mothers are strewn about the streets and terraces
Prostrate in their perplexity;
Nor have we got, nor do we expect to get,
Help from the Italian pope
Much less a visit;
I say like lava but sometimes like fire itself;
Last week our most distinguished seminarian
A student of the classics and a most courteous creature,
When he heard that his mother had been written to by the rector
About her son's ecumenical views
And that it had been arranged for her to pay her son a visit,
The gangling boy climbed up the fire-escape to the top-most roof-top
Sheer above the river far below
And launching himself off into space
Broke himself into smithereens upon the water's back.
Now peering down into his wat'ry grave
I think of what his young life might have been
If only pride of humility had obtained;
If Angelo Roncalli had paid a visit to this town

Rectors and bishops would have had to hightail it
And perhaps, God willing, they'd have never come back;
'As does any other man on earth
I come from a family and from a particular place';
But Roncalli is no more paid heed to
Than Gregory the Great
And the reign of Pius XII has been resumed –
He of the telephone and the solitary table
And the electric razor and the single-seater gold-plated cadillac;
Like some vast museum of a declining empire
The seminary is falling down

Prayer Street

The noise in Prayer Street is something awful:
Oh God.

What is a Protestant, Daddy?

Gaiters were sinister
And you dared not
Glance up at the visage;
With a crooked nose
And beaked dry lips
And streaky grey hair
And they used scurry about
In small black cars
(Unlike Catholic bishops
Stately in big cars
Or Pope Pius XII
In his gold-plated cadillac)
And they'd make dashes for it
Across deserted streets
And disappear quickly
Into vast cathedrals
All silent and aloof,
Forlorn and leafless,
Their belfry louvres
Like dead men's lips,
And whose congregation, if any,
Were all octogenarian

172

With names like Iris;
More likely
There were no congregations
And these rodent-like clergymen
Were conspirators;
You could see it in their faces;
But as to what the conspiracies
Were about, as children
We were at a loss to know;
Our parents called them 'parsons'
Which turned them from being rodents
Into black hooded crows
Evilly flapping their wings
About our virginal souls;
And these 'parsons' had wives –
As unimaginable a state of affairs
As it would have been to imagine
A pope in a urinal;
Protestants were Martians
Light-years more weird
Than zoological creatures;
But soon they would all go away
For as a species they were dying out,
Soon there would be no more Protestants. . .
O Yea, O Lord,
I was a proper little Irish Catholic boy
Way back in the 1950s.

The Haulier's Wife Meets Jesus
on the Road near Moone

I live in the town of Cahir,
In the Glen of Aherlow,
Not far from Peekaun
In the townland of Toureen,
At the foot of Galtee Mor
In the County of Tipperary.
I am thirty-three years old,
In the prime of my womanhood:
The mountain stream of my sex
In spate and darkly foaming;
The white hills of my breasts

Brimful and breathing:
The tall trees of my eyes
Screening blue skies;
Yet in each palm of my hand
A sheaf of fallen headstones.
When I stand in profile
Before my bedroom mirror
With my hands on my hips in my slip,
Proud of my body,
Unashamed of my pride,
I appear to myself a naked stranger,
A woman whom I do not know
Except fictionally in the looking-glass,
Quite dramatically beautiful.
Yet in my soul I yearn for affection,
My soul is empty for the want of affection.
I am married to a haulier,
A popular and a wealthy man,
An alcoholic and a county councillor,
Father by me of four sons,
By repute a sensitive man and he is
Except when he makes love to me:
He takes leave of his senses,
Handling me as if I were a sack of gravel,
Or a carnival dummy,
A fruit machine or a dodgem.
He makes love to me about twice a year;
Thereafter he does not speak to me for weeks,
Sometimes not for months.
One night in Cruise's Hotel in Limerick
I whispered to him: Please *take* me.
(We had been married five years
And we had two children.)
Christ, do you know what he said?
Where? Where do you want me to take you?
And he rolled over and fell asleep,
Tanked up with seventeen pints of beer.
We live in a Georgian, Tudor, Classical Greek,
Moorish, Spanish Hacienda, Regency Period,
Ranch-House, Three Storey Bungalow
On the edge of the edge of town:
'Poor Joe's Row' –
The townspeople call it –

174

But our real address is 'Ronald Reagan Hill',
– That vulturous-looking man in the States.
We're about twelve miles from Ballyporeen
Or, as the vulture flies, about eight miles.
After a month or two of silence
He says to me: Wife, I'm sorry;
I know that we should be separated,
Annulled or whatever,
But on account of the clients and the neighbours,
Not to mention the children, it is plain
As a pikestaff we are glued to one another
Until death do us part.
Why don't you treat yourself
To a week-end up in Dublin,
A night out at the theatre:
I'll pay for the whole shagging lot.
There was a play on at the time
In the Abbey Theatre in Dublin
Called *The Gigli Concert,*
And, because I liked the name –
But also because it starred
My favourite actor, Tom Hickey –
I telephoned the Abbey from Cahir,
They had but one vacant seat left!
I was so thrilled with myself,
And at the prospect of Tom Hickey
In a play called *The Gigli Concert*
(Such a euphonious name for a play),
That one wet day I drove over to Clonmel
And I went wild, and I bought a whole new oufit,
I am not one bit afraid to say
That I spent all of £200 on it
(Not, of course, that Tom Hickey would see me
But I'd be seeing myself seeing Tom Hickey
Which would be almost, if not quite,
The very next best thing):
A long, tight-fitting, black skirt
Of Chinese silk,
With matching black jacket
And lace-frilled pearl-white blouse;
Black fish-net stockings with sequins;
Black stiletto high-heeled shoes
Of pure ostrich leather.

I thought to myself – subconsciously, of course –
If I don't transpose to be somebody's *femme fatale*
It won't anyhow be for the want of trying.

Driving up to Dublin I began to day dream
And either at Horse & Jockey or Abbeyleix
I took a wrong turn and within a quarter-of-an-hour
I knew I was lost. I stopped the car
And I asked the first man I saw on the road
For directions:
'Follow me' – he said – 'my name is Jesus:
Have no fear of me – I am a travelling actor.
We'll have a drink together in the nearby inn.'
It turned out we were on the road near Moone
(Have you ever been to the Cross at Moone?
Once my children and I had a picnic at Moone
When they were little and we were on one
Of our Flight into Egypt jaunts to Dublin.
They ran round the High Cross round and round
As if it were a maypole, which maybe it is:
Figure carvings of loaves and fishes, lions and dolphins.
I drank black coffee from a thermos flask
and the children drank red lemonade
And they were wearing blue duffle coats with red scarves
And their small round laughing freckled faces
Looked exactly like the faces of the twelve apostles
Gazing out at us from the plinth of the Cross
Across a thousand years.
Only, of course, their father was not with us:
He was busy – busy being our family euphemism.
Every family in Ireland has its own family euphemism
Like a heraldic device or a coat of arms.)
Jesus turned out to be a lovely man,
All that a woman could ever possibly dream of:
Gentle, wild, soft-spoken, courteous, sad;
Angular, awkward, candid, methodical;
Humorous, passionate, angry, kind;
Entirely sensitive to a woman's world.
Discreetly I invited Jesus to spend the night with me –
Stay with me, the day is almost over and it is getting dark –
But he waved me aside with one wave of his hand,
Not contemptuously, but compassionately.
'Our night will come' he smiled,

And he resumed chatting about my children,
All curiosity for their welfare and well-being.
It was like a fire burning in me when he talked to me.
There was only one matter I felt guilty about
And that was my empty vacant seat in the Abbey.
At closing-time he kissed me on both cheeks
And we bade one another Goodbye and then –
Just as I had all but given up hope –
He kissed me full on the mouth,
My mouth wet with aziliran lipstick
(A tube of Guerlaine 4 which I've had for twelve years).
As I drove on into Dublin to the Shelbourne Hotel
I kept hearing his Midlands voice
Saying to me over and over, across the Garden of Gethsemane –
Our night will come.

Back in the town of Cahir,
In the Glen of Aherlow,
Not far from Peekaun
In the townland of Toureen,
At the foot of Galtee Mor
In the County of Tipperary,
For the sake of something to say
In front of our four sons
My husband said to me:
Well, what was Benjamino Gigli like?
Oh, 'twas a phenomenal concert!
And what was Tom Hickey like?
Miraculous – I whispered – miraculous.
Our night will come – he had smiled – our night will come.

PAUL MURRAY (1947-   )

Introit

This morning,
on entering the cold chapel,

I looked first
to the sun, as the pagan does,
not by strict custom
nor by constraint, but because

I too, as creature,
sense man's primitive emotion:
his need to praise.
And so, like priest or pagan,

            according
as the sun moves, I perform
this ancient ritual.
And though not always able

        to approach,
often, effaced in light, I stand
before this
chalice of the morning,

            I break this
ordinary bread as something holy.

Lauds

All things the Lord has made, O bless the Lord,
  Give glory and eternal praise to Him. . .

Together with our morning papers' dead:
unsmiling heroes, war-jaded, no longer game, the old,
the maimed, you also, your stoic gaiety
now needed more than ritual,

                        O bless the Lord.

And you, and you also,
crazed victims of unnatural love, chained to
the masks of vampire or sacrificial dove,
the tortured and the torturer,
                    O bless the Lord.

And you, who have no fear
of those who crush the bone, your innocence inviolable;
stone angel, prostrate in your mother's womb,
unwanted three-months' miracle,

                        O bless the Lord.

And buried behind charitable walls,
the unseen, unmourned for, you, your voices ever singing

178

in the darkness, cherubim of dwarf and mongol, bright
galaxy of souls of Limbo,

                         O bless the Lord.

And you, the hideously mourned, lips
parted, rouged, smiling under expensive oils, O Dives
when through the painted mask
your lips are burned,

                         O bless the Lord.

And you, when on your brow there glows
the desolate mark of Cain, when in your eyes, in the temple
of your heart, only the towering and dead
effigies of God remain,

                         O bless the Lord.

And you, whose memory revives
after the serpent sting: eyes closed, imagining your soul
redeemed, re-entering the lost kingdom. Exile,
when Death shall prove your dream,

                         O bless the Lord.

And you, those dying under ritual of torture
or no ritual: the suicides, the uncremated spirits in the fires
of Purgatory and Buchenwald – O quiet, innumerable
souls facing unquiet doom,

now, out of the burning fiery furnace,
out of the heart of the flame,

       give glory and eternal praise to Him.

from *Meditations*

III

With those friends who disclaim all knowledge
of God, I boast and I say,

                     'I know Him',
and I say I am speaking from my own experience.
But my friends say: 'Be reasonable, how
can you know Him, how can you be so sure
that you are not self-deceived?' This question,

I know, is honest; and I know it demands
for an answer not these obscure words
about experience, but the clear evidence
of a man's life. However, I will say it
here again, and even to my own doubting heart,
and to my five agnostic senses: 'I know Him'.

VII

Sometimes when I speak to you,
                                        Lord,
my friends tell me I am foolish, or that
I am dreaming. And maybe
they are not completely mistaken. For it is
true that you have given me a life
which is a kind of sleep,
and that everything I now perceive
appears for the most part
                                        like a dream.
And so, 'Yes', I will say to my friends, 'He
is, of course, part of my dream, but then
I am part of his dream, too'.

IX

Not the naked sudden thought
of this or that lovely girl,
the sudden impulse, the desire to take
into my arms for a brief moment
the sensual, midnight spouse.
Not that which in the mind is natural
to imagine, natural to affirm: the most
ordinary, most obvious answer
to a grown man's fullest need.
Not that calmness therefore, not even
with the trembling of desire appeased,
that dark spontaneous joining together
in one flesh, of man and woman,
that brief perfect equilibrium.
And yet, at times, I know that in my
being you have touched me, Lord:
the stark passion of desire
is calmed, and calm is passionate.

To raise up from the ground my whole being
and my life; each day, with my hands empty,
and my heart empty, to stand, and to look
towards the one source of all.

    To be able to accept the hour of knowing
and of unknowing, to be able to be passive.
And though not yet by this or by that vow
made naked in my intent, to be, through time,
by one desire, one gift, made careless
of every covering and of every cloth. Not by
atonement of will, but by His power, to be able
to lie down passive like Michelangelo's Adam.

    O to feel, at the tip of my finger, God's
suddenly light pressure, that same merciless,
merciful lightning of God's hand.

GERARD SMYTH (1951-   )

Temple

I

Whose eyes are these that gaze and gaze
from sculpted solitude
– fading from icon and pieta?

It is getting dark.
Dusk has half-erased the house of God.
From nowhere comes the voice
of supplication, pleading
at the edge of light and refuge.

Out of the depths and from echoing hill
earth's cries
invoke the unsealed sepulchre
    where death consoles the living.

II

Silencing all questions
the smoke of incense hoists a chant
of joyous Easter Latin.

Brass and bronze have the appearance of gold.
The bones of statues
are radiant in light from another world.

The entry door looms up –
when it opens the air divides,
wisps of air breathe down the nave
of brooding quietness.

Stone rises to reach the sky.
Where sunlight collides with chapel glass
a hermit stands in fire
reciting, perhaps, the last of the psalms.

PAUL MULDOON (1951-   )

Our Lady of Ardboe

I

Just there, in a corner of the whin-field,
Just where the thistles bloom.
She stood there as in Bethlehem
One night in nineteen fifty-three or four.

The girl leaning over the half-door
Saw the cattle kneel, and herself knelt.

II

I suppose that a farmer's youngest daughter
Might, as well as the next, unravel
The winding road to Christ's navel.

Who's to know what's knowable?
Milk from the Virgin Mother's breast,
A feather off the Holy Ghost?
The fairy thorn? The holy well?

Our simple wish for there being more to life
Than a job, a car, a house, a wife –
The fixity of running water.

For I like to think, as I step these acres,
That a holy well is no more shallow
Nor plummetless than the pools of Shiloh,
The fairy thorn no less true than the Cross.

III
Mother of our Creator, Mother of our Saviour,
Mother most amiable, Mother most admirable,
Virgin most prudent, Virgin most venerable,
Mother inviolate, Mother undefiled.

And I walk waist-deep among purples and golds
With one arm as long as the other.

BIOGRAPHIES

AE (George William Russell) (1867-1935) born in the North of Ireland, established a branch of the Theosophical Society in Dublin. Known as a mystic and a man of business, he edited *The Irish Homestead,* organ of the Agricultural Co-operative Society. He was also known as a painter. Spent time as editor of *The Irish Statesman* and did extensive lecture tours of America.

WILLIAM ALLINGHAM (1824-1889) born in Ballyshannon, Co Donegal but moved to London where he became a professional man of letters. He was prominent in pre-Raphaelite circles and was editor of *Fraser's Magazine.* His work generally centred on the Irish countryside, on old ballad metres, and on popular traditions. He died in London.

JEREMIAH JOSEPH CALLANAN (1795-1829) born in Cork, studied for the priesthood for a time, then studied to be a doctor. He wandered about Ireland a great deal and died of tuberculosis in Portugal. His poem, 'The Outlaw of Loch Lene' had a very strong influence on the development of Irish cadences in poetry.

JOSEPH CAMPBELL (1879-1944) born in Belfast, a member of the insurrectionary group of 1916 but did not take an active part in the insurrection. He was imprisoned by the Free State Government. Later went to America and founded a school of Irish studies there. On his return to Ireland he lived in a hillside cottage outside Dublin. Many of his poems have become popular folk songs.

AUSTIN CLARKE (1896-1974) born in Dublin, early influence of Yeats soon overcome. Reacted to the restrictions of the Church and his poetry became strongly satirical. Lived in London for a time, then settled in Templeogue, Dublin.

PADRAIG J DALY (1943-) born in Dungarvan, Co Waterford. Joined the Augustinian Order in 1960 and works as a priest with the order in Dublin. A large selection of his poetry has been published in Italy. He is a frequent broadcaster on Radio Eireann.

JOHN F DEANE (1943-) born on Achill Island, Co Mayo. Taught in Dublin for several years and in 1979 resigned to devote his time to poetry, and to developing Poetry Ireland, the poetry society he founded in 1978. Is editor of *The Dedalus Press*. Has published several collections.

SEAMUS DEANE (1940-) born in Derry, educated at St Columb's College, Queen's University, Belfast, and Cambridge University; is Professor of English Literature at University College, Dubin, and lecturers occasionally in America. Won the AE Memorial Award.

DENIS DEVLIN (1908-1959) born in Greenock, Scotland, came to Ireland at the age of ten. Schooled at Belvedere College; studied in a seminary for some time, but left and went to University College, Dublin. Studied at the Universities of Munich and the Sorbonne. Taught for a time in English Department of University College, Dublin, and then entered a career with the Department of External Affairs, serving in Rome, New York, Washington, London.

PAUL DURCAN (1944-) born in Dublin and has lived in Cork. One of the most individual voices of his generation, he has published many collections of poetry. In 1982 Blackstaff Press published his *The Selected Paul Durcan*. They have also published *The Berlin Wall Café* (1985), *Going home to Russia* (1987), *Jesus and Angela* (1988) and *Daddy, Daddy* (*1990).

JOHN ENNIS (1944-) born in Westmeath, a graduate of the University College Cork and Dublin, he won the Patrick Kavanagh Award in 1975. Now lives in Waterford where he is a lecturer in the Regional College.

KEVIN FALLER (1920-1983) born in Galway City, worked in Dublin with publishers and newspapers since 1945. Numerous radio plays produced. His *Selected Poems* was published in 1982.

PADRAIC FALLON (1905-1974) born in Athenry, Co Galway. Drawn by AE into the Irish Literary Revival, he wrote stories, articles and radio plays. Worked for many years as a civil servant. Did not publish a book until 1974.

ROBERT FARREN (1909-1985) born in Dublin. School teacher and director of broadcasting in Radio Eireann for many years. His critical work *The Course of Irish Poetry* was much acclaimed.

SAMUEL FERGUSON (1810-1886) born in Belfast, died in Howth, Co Dublin. His *Lays of the Western Gael* and *Congal* helped develop the movement that began with Yeats in the 1880s. His translations of Gaelic folk songs brought the Gaelic rhythms into verse in English. An antiquarian, he later became president of the Royal Irish Academy, and was knighted.

PADRAIC FIACC (1924-) born in Belfast and lived in New York for some years where he became acquainted with Padraic Colum. Won the AE Memorial Award and has published an influential anthology on violence in the North, *The Wearing of the Black,* Blackstaff Press 1974.

MONK GIBBON (1896-1987) born in Dublin. Served as an officer in France during World War I. Invalided out in 1918 he went to Switzerland to teach. Travelled widely. Published several collections of poetry and is known as novelist, biographer and essayist. Lived in Dublin.

MICHAEL HARTNETT (1941-) born in Co Limerick and lived for a time in London, Dublin and Madrid before settling in Limerick in 1974. Has translated from the Spanish of Lorca and from the *Tao,* and has translated some contemporary Irish poetry into English. In 1975 he announced his intention of writing only in Irish.

FRANCIS HARVEY (1925-) born in Co Fermanagh and has lived most of his life in Co Donegal where he worked as a banker. Has written several radio plays. He has published two collections of poetry with The Gallery Press.

SEAMUS HEANEY (1939-) born in Co Derry, educated at St Columb's College, Derry, and at Queen's University, Belfast. Has held various teaching posts and was appointed Oxford Professor of Poetry in 1989.

JOHN HEWITT (1907-1987) born in Belfast, educated at Methodist College and Queen's University. In 1930 appointed Art Assistant at the Belfast Museum and Art Gallery and later became Deputy Director. In 1957 moved to a post in Coventry, retiring in 1972 and returning to Belfast.

F R HIGGINS (1896-1941) born in Mayo and spent much of his life in Co Meath. He was director of the Abbey Theatre from 1935 until his untimely death. A protegee of Yeats for some years.

PEARSE HUTCHINSON (1927-) was Gregory Fellow in Poetry at the University of Leeds, 1971 to 1973. Has presented radio programmes and lives in Dublin where he is co-editor of the literary review *Cyphers.* Gallery Press has published his *Selected Poems.*

JOHN KELLS INGRAM (1823-1907) born in Donegal and died in Dublin. Became a professor in Trinity College. His best-known poem is 'The Memory of the Dead' which he published in the *Nation* as a student. Later much influenced by the positivism of Auguste Comte, and scared of the implications of his earlier ballad.

PATRICK KAVANAGH (1904-1967) born in Monaghan, lived in Dublin for some thirty years. Wrote novels, drama and poetry and has had a unique effect on Irish poetry.

RICHARD KELL (1927-) born in Cork. After five years in India he attended schools in Belfast and Dublin, graduating from Trinity College. Worked as librarian and teacher in England until his appointment to the post of Senior Lecturer in English Literature at Newcastle-upon-Tyne Polytechnic.

BRENDAN KENNELLY (1936-) born in Co Kerry. Educated in Tarbert and Trinity College Dublin, and Leeds University. Has published many collections of poetry and edited the *Penguin Book of Irish Verse*. Author of two novels, he was awarded the Irish Critics Harvey's award for his play *Medea* (1988) and edited *Landmarks in Irish Drama* (Methuen). Is Professor of Modern Literature in Trinity College, Dublin.

JEROME KIELY (1925-) born in Kinsale, educated at diocesan college in Cork and St Patrick's College, Maynooth. Ordained a priest in 1950. Works as a priest in Co Cork. Won the Adam Prize for poetry in 1956.

THOMAS KINSELLA (1928-) born in Dublin. Spends part of the time as a lecturer in America and the rest of the year in Wicklow. The Peppercannister Press publishes special editions of his work. One of the most influential of contemporary Irish poets.

FRANCIS LEDWIDGE (1891-1917) born in Co Meath. His work attracted the attention and patronage of Lord Dunsany. He joined the British Army early during the war and served in Greece. Was in Ireland during the 1916 Rising and very troubled by it but returned to the trenches where he was killed in 1917 in Flanders.

JAMES LIDDY (1934-) born in Clare. Works as a professor at the University of Wisconsin in America and returns regularly to Ireland. He has published several collections of poetry.

JAMES McAULEY (1936-) born in Dublin but has lived away from Ireland for many years and is now Professor of English at Eastern Washington University. He published a collection of poetry with The Dolmen Press.

ROY McFADDEN (1921-) born in Belfast. Became a solicitor and has remained working in Belfast. From 1948-53 he co-edited *Rann,* publishing work by local English and American poets. Has published eight collections, including *Letter to the Hinterland* (1986).

THOMAS D'ARCY McGEE (1825-1868) had to flee Ireland because of his activity with the Young Ireland group. Became Minister for Agriculture in Canada where he was assassinated.

FRANCIS MacMANUS (1909-1965) best known as a novelist; he published one collection of poetry.

LOUIS MacNEICE (1907-1963) born in Belfast, educated at Marlborough and Merton College, Oxford; the son of a Bishop of the Church of Ireland. A classical scholar, he lectured for a time in Classics at Birmingham and London. In 1941 he joined the BBC and worked in radio there.

EWART MILNE (1903-1984) born in Dublin. In 1923 became a Merchant Navy cadet. Trips to Africa, Calcutta, New York. Worked at various jobs. In 1936 went to Spain where he worked as medical courier. Lived in England with a short spell in Ireland. In 1983 Aquila published a Festschrift for his 80th birthday.

DEREK MAHON (1941-) born in Belfast, educated at Trinity College, Dublin, and has been living in London where for a time he was literary editor of *The New Statesman*. He has won many awards for his poetry.

JOHN MONTAGUE (1929-) born in New York and has lived in America and France. Now lives in Ireland and holds a teaching post in Albany, New York. His most recent collection of poems is *Mount Eagle*, Gallery Press.

PAUL MULDOON (1951-) born in Armagh, he now lives in the United States. He has published five collections of poems with Faber & Faber.

RICHARD MURPHY (1927-) born in Galway and lived for a time in India. He has spent several seasons in Sri Lanka and a collection of poems *The Mirror Wall* (Wolfhound) has come from these visits. In 1989 Faber published a substantial new *Selected Poems*. Now living in Dublin.

PAUL MURRAY (1947-) born in Newcastle, Co Down, educated in Belfast. He entered the Dominican Order in 1966. Teaches at the Dominican Studium in Tallaght, Co Dublin.

DESMOND O'GRADY (1935-) born in Limerick. Lived in and travelled Europe, the Middle East and America. Worked for a time with Ezra Pound. Now living in Kinsale, Co Cork. He has published several collections with Gallery Press.

JOHN BOYLE O'REILLY (1844-1890) a prominent Fenian, he was sentenced to twenty years' penal servitude in Australia, but escaped and went to America where in 1876 he became part-owner of a Boston newspaper.

JOSEPH MARY PLUNKETT (1887-1916) born in Dublin and was one of the leaders of the insurrection of 1916. He was executed after the surrender, with his colleagues Padraig Pearse and Thomas MacDonagh.

W R RODGERS (1909-1969) born in Belfast and was a friend of Louis

MacNeice. Graduate of Queen's University, was student in the Assembly College and was called in 1934 to the Presbyterian Church at Loughgall, Co Armagh. In 1946 he joined the Features Department of the BBC in London, where he worked until 1952.

JAMES SIMMONS (1933-) born in Derry and educated at Leeds University. Has written his own songs and performed them on radio, disc and television. Lectured in the English Department of the New University of Ulster, Coleraine.

GERARD SMYTH (1951-) born in Dublin. Works as journalist with *The Irish Times*. He has published three full collections of poetry. The most recent being *Painting the Pink Roses Black* (Dedalus Press).

JAMES STEPHENS (1882-1950) published *The Charwoman's Daughter* in the *Irish Review* of which he was one of the editors, and which launched him on a highly successful writing career.

JOHN MILLINGTON SYNGE (1871-1909) graduated from Dublin University and went to the continent to study music. Lived in Paris before coming back to learn Irish and the local dialects of English. Wrote a series of powerful plays.

JOHN TODHUNTER (1839-1916) born in Dublin and taught in Alexandra College for some time before moving to London where he practised medicine and wrote plays, including a translation of Faust. In London he helped found the Irish Literary Society.

KATHERINE TYNAN (1861-1931) born in Dublin. Wrote several volumes of reminiscences of life in Ireland and England in the 1890s and 1900s. Died in London.

RICHARD WEBER (1932-) born in Dublin. He has published several slim volumes and three full collections, *Lady and Gentleman, Stephen's Green Revisited*. and *A Few Small Ones*. Has lived and lectured abroad but now lives in Dublin and works in the National College of Art & Design.

OSCAR WILDE (1854-1900) born in Dublin, son of Sir William Wilde; his mother wrote poetry for the *Nation* under the name Speranza.

WILLIAM BUTLER YEATS (1865-1939) born in Dublin, died in France. Began to write in the tradition of Allingham and Ferguson, but developed his own interests and style, helped by Ezra Pound and T S Eliot. Through his efforts the Abbey Theatre was created. On the establishment of the Irish Free State he became a senator. Was awarded the Nobel Prize for Literature.

Acknowledgements

For permission to reprint poems in this anthology, we would like to acknowledge the following with thanks. For poems by: Joseph Campbell from *The Poems of Joseph Campbell*, Simon D. Campbell. Austin Clarke from *Collected Poems*, R. Dardis Clarke. Padraig J. Daly from *A Celibate Affair* and *Nowhere But in Praise*, the author. John F. Deane from *High Sacrifice* and *Winter in Meath*, the author. Seamus Deane from *Rumours*, the author. Denis Devlin, the author. Paul Durcan from *Sam's Cross, Berlin Wall Café* and *Selected Paul Durcan*, Blackstaff Press. John Ennis from *Night on Hibernia*, Gallery Press. Kevin Faller from *Memoirs*, Una Faller. Padraic Fallon from *Poems and Versions* and *Poems*, Brian Fallon. Robert Farren from *Selected Poems*, Ronan Farren. Padraic Fiacc from *The Wearing of the Black/Nights in the Bad Place*, Blackstaff Press. Monk Gibbon, the Legal Executor of the Estate of Monk Gibbon. Michael Hartnett from *Collected Poems*, Raven Arts Press. Francis Harvey from *In the Light on the Stones*, Gallery Press. Seamus Heaney from *Death of a Naturalist*, Faber and Faber Limited. John Hewitt from *Out of My Time, Collected Poems* and *Kites in Spring*, Blackstaff Press. F.R. Higgins from *The Dark Bread* and *The Gap of Brightness*, the Legal Executor of the Estate of F.R. Higgins. Pearse Hutchinson from *The Frost is All Over*, Gallery Press; and from *Expansions/Tongue without Hands*, the author. Patrick Kavanagh from *Lough Derg, Collected Poems* and *The Great Hunger*, Gallery Press. Richard Kell from *Control Tower*, Chatto & Windus; and from *The Broken Circle*, the author. Brendan Kennelly from *The Boats are Home*, the author. Jerome Kiely from *The Griffin Sings*, the author. Thomas Kinsella from *Moralities, Another September, Downstream* and *Nightwalker and Other Poems*, the author. Thomas Kinsella from *Moralities, Another September, Downstream* and *Nightwalker and Other Poems*, the author. James Liddy from *In a Blue Smoke* and *Blue Mountain*, the author. James McAuley from *Draft Balance Sheet*, the author. Roy McFadden from *The Garryowen*, the author. Francis MacManus from *Pedlar's Pack*, Patrick MacManus, Louis MacNeice, Faber and Faber Limited. Derek Mahon from *Poems 1962-1978*, Oxford University Press. Ewart Milne from *Galion* and *Cantata under Orion*, Kevin Milne. John Montague from *Selected Poems*, the author. Paul Muldoon from *Mules*, the author. Richard Murphy from *New Selected Poems*, Faber and Faber Limited. Paul Murray from *Rites and Meditations*, the author. Desmond O'Grady from *The Dark Edge of Europe*, the author. W.R. Rodgers from *Collected Poems*, Martin Secker & Warburg Limited. James Simmons from *Constantly Singing*, Gallery Press. Gerard Smyth from *Painting the Pink Roses Black*, the author. James Stephens from *Collected Poems*, the Society of Authors on behalf of the Estate of James Stephens. Richard Weber from *Stephen's Green Revisited*, the author.

In the case of a few poems we have been unable to make contact with copyright holders, and we would be grateful if they would contact the publisher.

Index of Authors

Numbers refer to pages